Movie Dinners

First published in the United Kingdom in 2010 by
Portico Books
10 Southcombe Street
London
W14 0RA

An imprint of Anova Books Company Ltd

ISBN 9781906032869

A CIP catalogue record for this book is available from the British Library.

10 9 8 7 6 5 4 3 2 1

Printed and bound by 1010 Printing International Ltd, China

This book can be ordered direct from the publisher at www.anovabooks.com

For more information about Becky, and her recipes, please visit www.beckythorn.me.uk

Movie Dinners

by

Becky Thorn

Reel Recipes From Your Favourite Films

PORTICO

The Cast

INTRODUCTION 008

THE DIRECTOR'S CUT

Mint Julep
Gone With the Wind 014
Two Whisky Sours (and a peanut butter sandwich)
The Seven Year Itch 016
Champagne and Strawberries
Pretty Woman 018
Chocolate Martini
Atonement 020
Cosmopolitan
Sex and the City 022
Afternoon Tea
Brief Encounter 024
Gibson
All About Eve 026
Pan Galactic Gargleblaster
The Hitchhiker's Guide to the Galaxy 028
Martini
Goldfinger 030
White Russian
The Big Lebowski 032
Velvet Hammer
Cocktail 034
A Selection of Wine
Sideways 036

More Movie Drinks
More drinks to enjoy with your favourite films 038

SHORTS

Bantha Milkshake
Star Wars 042
Blue Soup
Bridget Jones' Diary 044
50 Hard Boiled Eggs / Raw Egg Smoothie
Cool Hand Luke / Rocky 046
Crab Dumplings
Eat Drink Man Woman 048
Fish Ceviche
A Fish Called Wanda 050
French Toast
Kramer Vs Kramer 052
Small Bread Sandwiches
Spinal Tap 054
Turkey Sandwich
When Harry Met Sally 056
Chilli Cheese Dogs
Dragnet 058

MAIN FEATURE

Big Kahuna Burger
Pulp Fiction 062

Cannoli
The Godfather 064

Lobster
Annie Hall 066

Boeuf Bourguignon
Julie & Julia 068

Calamari
Shirley Valentine 070

Chicken Mole
Chicken Mole 072

Lasagna
Garfield 074

My Big Fat Greek Wedding
Lemon Lamb 076

Liver, Fava Beans (and a Nice Chianti)
Silence of the Lambs 078

Meatloaf
Pleasantville 080

Meat Pie
Sweeeney Todd 082

Pancakes, Bacon and Syrup
Groundhog Day 084

Pease Pudding and Saveloy
Oliver! 086

Pierogi
Men In Black 088

Pizza
Mystic Pizza 090

Rabbit Stew
Fatal Attraction 092
Roast Quail
Babette's Feast 094
Scallops with Saffron Sauce
No Reservations 096
Seafood Risotto
Big Night 098
Sizzling Steak
The Devil Wears Prada 100
Mama Joe's Cornbread
Soul Food 102
Spaghetti Sauce with Wafer Thin Garlic and Meatballs
Goodfellas.. 104
Roast Venison
Deer Hunter... 106
Thanksgiving Dinner
Planes, Trains and Automobiles 108
Poutine
Diner 110

SEQUELS

Apple Pie
American Pie 114
Apple Strudel
The Sound of Music 116
Baked Beans
Blazing Saddles 118

Bruce Bogtrotter's Chocolate Cake
Matilda 120
Chocolate Fondue
Willy Wonka and the Chocolate Factory 122
Chocolate Mousse
Rosemary's Baby 124
Strawberry Chocolate Pie
Waitress 126
Crème Brûlée
Amelie 128
Custard Pie
Battle of the Century 130
Jelly
9 1/2 Weeks 132
Gelato
Roman Holiday 134
Pecan Pie
Hairspray 136
Mash
M* A* S* H* 138

OUT-TAKES

Cherryade Chocolate Float
Grease 142
Chicken Salad Sandwich
Five Easy Pieces 144
Four Fried Chicken (and some dry white toast)
The Blues Brothers 146

Fried Green Tomatoes
Fried Green Tomatoes 148
The Ipcress File
Green Pepper Omelette 150
Bhajis and Pakora
Bend It Like Beckham 152
Turkish Delight
The Lion, The Witch and The Wardrobe 154
Wafer-thin Mints
Monty Python's Meaning of Life 156
The World's Best Sandwich
Spanglish 158
Twinkies
Ghostbusters 160

TV DINNERS

Donuts
The Simpsons 164
Chef's Chocolate Salty Balls
South Park 166
French Fries
Happy Days 168
Phoebe's Grandma's Cookies
Friends 170

BONUS FEATURES 172

OSCAR ACCEPTANCE SPEECH 174

Introduction

The prospect of dinner and a movie is always an enticing one. Whether it is an apprehensive and frisson-filled date early on in a relationship, or the opportunity for a relaxing child-free evening and a chance to watch something of your choice all the way through, the combination of food and film is always a winner.

Food is inextricably linked to all aspects of our daily lives: food to share, food to comfort, food to harm and, of course, food to raise the sexual tension — and cinematographers know this too. Frequently there are dishes in a movie that deserve as much of a mention in the credits as the cast. Sylvester Stallone's Rocky, after downing his raw egg smoothie, did little for egg sales but everyone who watched the movie immediately had the utmost respect for a man who would willingly drink something so vile to prove he's got what it takes to be champion. You only have to mention *Silence of the Lambs* for 'fava beans and a nice chianti' to spring into the conversation, followed by a sinister and no doubt rubbish impersonation of Anthony Hopkins! And, of course, how could we forget, the Big Kahuna burger from *Pulp Fiction* that leads Samuel L Jackson into a killing spree. It just looks to die for, doesn't it?

However, it's not only the directors who influence the inclusion of food in a movie. Brad Pitt's constant grazing habits were incorporated into *Ocean's Eleven* as a constant narrative device. Pitt's character Rusty Ryan is so caught up with pulling off the Las Vegas mega-heist that he and the gang never sit down to eat a proper meal, so he eats on the go. This was a neat little trick pulled by the director Steven Soderbergh and Rusty's scoffing of fast food came to symbolise the fast speed at which the story unravels. Miss it? Go back and watch it again!

Let us get one thing straight here: The delectable dishes celebrated in this book are not available at your local multiplex cinema concession stands. Gloopy nachos and fluffy hotdogs are not what this book is about. These lovingly made recipes are for those movie moments that made you look away from the popcorn bucket, and up at the big screen and think 'Ooh, I bet that tastes *amazing!*'

After all, who wouldn't be tempted to slice garlic with a razor blade to re-create Paulie's infamous, garlicky, spaghetti sauce in *Goodfellas*, or jump through the screen to nibble absolutely everything in *Willy Wonka's Chocolate Factory* and, of course, what women doesn't want 'what she's having' after having watched that diner scene in *When Harry Met Sally*!

Well, now you can. If it was eaten on screen in your favourite movie then the recipe may well be in this book. Unless you fancy making the chilled monkey brains from *Indiana Jones and the Temple of Doom* — in which case I suggest you still buy the book but change your dessert plans and make a crisp apple strudel from *The Sound of Music* instead.

Tuck in and enjoy!

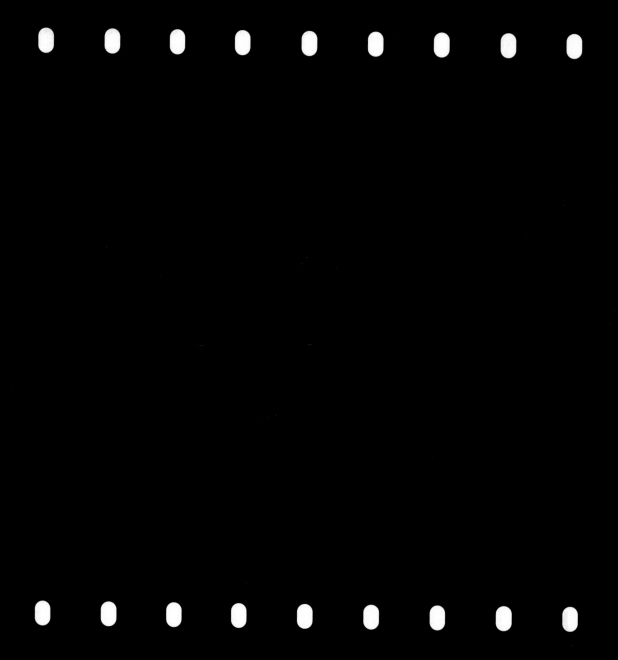

The Director's Cut

The perfect accompaniment to any movie.
Please try and drink responsibly...

*'I'm very drunk and I intend on getting still drunker
before this evening's over'*

[CAST & CREW]

a good handful of mint
  leaves
15ml (¹/₂ fl oz) sugar
  syrup
crushed ice
50ml (2fl oz) bourbon
sparkling or soda water,
  chilled

Serves 1

Watching *Gone With the Wind* taught me much as a
teenage girl – how to flounce, how to use the phrase
'fiddle dee dee' in context, and that no woman should
show her bosom before 3pm.

Scarlett O'Hara is a spoiled, contrary and
manipulative woman but despite all that she also has
a backbone of steel and a healthy drinking habit. At
one point in the film she even gargles with eau de
cologne to get rid of her bourbon breath. Classy!

Now don't you go that far. Instead, just offer your
guests a delicious mint julep so that you can all
have that ring of confidence and fresh minty breath.

[VOICE-OVER]

To make a simple sugar syrup pour equal quantities by volume of sugar and water in a heavy-bottomed pan. Heat gently until the sugar dissolves, then heat until boiling. Boil for 5 minutes and then leave to cool. To make mint syrup put a bunch of fresh mint leaves in a bowl and pour over the hot syrup. Leave to infuse until the syrup is cold. Strain and bottle the syrup. You can also buy mint syrup in most coffee shops. If you don't have time to make or buy the syrup, put 1 tsp icing sugar and 2 tsp water in each glass.

[MISE-EN-SCENE]

1. Pop the mint leaves into a tall glass and add the sugar syrup. Bruise the leaves gently using a mortar, rolling pin or back of a spoon to release the mint oils.

2. Fill the glass with crushed ice and stir again. Splash in the bourbon and top up with sparkling or soda water. (If you only have cold still water, that will do at a push.)

3. Stir again and set to one side. Do not think about sipping this until the glass has condensation on the outside. If you are somewhere with air conditioning, go outside to get the full benefit of this cooling beverage.

4. Repeat until the cooling effect kicks in. After all... tomorrow is another day.

Two Whisky Sours
and a Peanut Butter Sandwich

THE SEVEN YEAR ITCH (1955)

'Miss Morris, I'm perfectly capable of fixing my own breakfast. As a matter of fact, I had a peanut butter sandwich and two whiskey sours'

[CAST & CREW]

Sandwich
  2 slices bread
  butter for spreading
  peanut butter - smooth
    or crunchy
Whisky Sour
4 measures whisky
4 measures fresh lemon
  juice
2 measures simple sugar
  syrup
ice
2 orange slices
2 maraschino cherries

Serves 2

Marilyn Monroe's girl is ditsy and cute. Exactly the type of girl that Richard has sworn to avoid. As she classily dunks her potato chips into champagne the Rachmaninoff he plays on the piano has an effect. Exactly what effect? Well, you will have to watch the film to find out.

Just be careful though, 'When something itches, my dear sir, the natural tendency is to scratch.' Which is precisely how Marilyn, I bet, kept her figure with such an unhealthy diet!

This is a great movie for a Sunday afternoon, but I wouldn't recommend too many servings of either recipes listed right...

[VOICE-OVER]

If you want to give the Whisky Sour a frothy top then add in a dash of egg white at the shaking stage. This then becomes a Boston Sour but it does look very pretty and seductive - if that is your intention.

[MISE-EN-SCENE]

1. **Sandwich** - Place the bread onto a plate and butter both slices on one side only.

2. Open the jar of peanut butter. Liberally spread one of the buttered slices of bread with the peanut butter. The covering of peanut butter should be to a depth of approximately ¼ of an inch.

3. Place the second slice of bread down onto the peanut-buttered slice. The outside of the sandwich should be butter and peanut butter free. Squash the slices together but try not to allow the filling to ooze out.

4. If you have company cut the sandwich into halves or quarters. If you don't then what's the point!

5. **Whisky Sours** - Place some of the ice into acocktail shaker. Add in the fresh lemon, whisky and the simple syrup. Shake well.

6. Pour into a wide-mouthed tumbler if you have one. Garnish with half a slice of orange and a maraschino cherry. If you have the self-control you could listen to Rachmaninoff at the same time.

7. Eat a peanut butter sandwich, drink the second sour, pick up your laptop and off to work you go. It is breakfast after all.

Champagne & Strawberries

PRETTY WOMAN (1990)

'Look, I'll tell ya what. I'll be back. We'll do broccoli tomorrow'

[CAST & CREW]

1 bottle champagne
  (although prosecco will
  do at a push)
1 punnet large, ripe
  strawberries, at room
  temperature
1 $300 a night hooker
  (optional)

Serves 2

From a carpet picnic of champagne and strawberries to a night at the opera, Edward and Vivien share a week that changes both their lives forever and shows that no matter how rich or hard up you may be, everyone needs rescuing sometimes. And what better way to rescue someone than with champagne and strawberries!

Next time your partner tries to seduce you, hang on until they offer you this exotic combination. No one, not even an L.A. call girl like Vivien, wants to be a cheap date. Make sure you keep floss on hand though. Strawberry seeds are vicious little buggers.

[VOICE-OVER]

You could always pop a smaller strawberry into the glass before adding the champagne. This has the advantage of leaving one hand free for 'other' activities.

[MISE-EN-SCENE]

1. Call room service and place an order for a bottle of chilled champagne and a large punnet of ripe strawberries.

2. Open the door, tell the porter where to put the tray. Be generous with your tip.

3. Carefully uncork the champagne and slowly fill the flutes until two-thirds full. Never fill your champagne to the top of the glass - it's uncouth, don't you know!

4. Offer a glass of champagne with one hand and a strawberry with the other to prevent your guest downing the glass in one.

5. Repeat until your partner can't keep his hands off you.

Chocolate Martini

ATONEMENT (2007)

'Bite it... You've got to bite it...'

[CAST & CREW]

25ml (1fl oz) crème de
  cacao
100ml (4fl oz) vodka
chocolate-covered coffee
  bean

Serves 1

Robbie's rather raunchy missive devastates all those concerned and the fallout from his actions sends the whole story swirling into action.

Paul Marshall's character, the creator of this Chocolate Martini, wreaks havoc for everyone in the movie — but then maybe that's because he's drunk from his own creation a little too often!

This recipe is a little changed from the one in the book (and the movie) and errs towards the gloopy side.

Still, chocolate and Martini...what could possibly go wrong?

[VOICE-OVER]

If you do want to decorate the rim of the martini glasses, there are lots of possibilities. Dip the glass rims in melted chocolate and then chill until the chocolate sets. Alternatively, dip the rims in chocolate sauce, then cocoa, cocoa nibs or chocolate vermicelli. Space dust would bring a fun element to each mouthful. Or follow the trend for sea-salted chocolates and use salt to rim the chocolate-dipped glass?

[MISE—EN—SCENE]

1. Fill the shaker up with ice. Pour in the crème de cacao and vodka.

2. Shake well.

3. Strain into a chocolate-rimmed martini glass (see serving suggestion) and float a chocolate-covered bean on top.

4. Sip slowly, as this drink may cause you to do and say things you could regret if consumed at speed and in large quantities.

Cosmopolitan

SEX AND THE CITY (2008)

'So what are we going to do? Sit around bars, sipping Cosmos and sleeping with strangers when we're eighty?'

[CAST & CREW]

crushed ice
50ml (2fl oz) vodka
25ml (1fl oz) triple sec
15ml (½ fl oz) lime
  cordial
25ml (1fl oz) cranberry
  juice
lemon wedges, lime
  cheeks or orange peel
  twists, to garnish

Serves 1 (but never
drink one alone!)

There seem to be as many variations on the Cosmopolitan as positions in the Kama Sutra. Connoisseurs and bartenders have tinkered with the traditional recipe by adding flavoured vodkas, changing the triple sec for Cointreau or Grand Marnier, and even swapping the lime juice for lime cordial or lemon juice. However, I'm quite sure the SATC girls aren't that fussy about what's in it, as long as they keep flowing!

Whether you go for one straight up or lying down, the other essential ingredient in this recipe is the opportunity to spend an evening with close friends discussing men, shoes and cupcakes.

[VOICE-OVER]

Arguments rage over how to garnish this wonderful cocktail – lemon wedges, lime cheeks and flaming orange peel twists feature in recipes. One thing everyone does agree on is that this must be shaken over crushed ice and served in a martini glass, straight up.

[MISE-EN-SCENE]

1. Put on your Jimmy Choos if you have them, you lucky thing.

2. Half-fill a cocktail shaker with crushed ice.

3. Add in the measurements of vodka, triple sec, lime cordial and cranberry juice.

4. Shake and strain into a martini glass and garnish.

5. Repeat as necessary throughout the evening while discussing Mr Big - or his countless rivals.

Afternoon Tea

BRIEF ENCOUNTER (1945)

'Take your tea and be quiet'

[CAST & CREW]

1 large teapot (with
  hand-knitted cosy)
3 spoonfuls of leaf tea
  (one per person and one
  for the pot)
Boiling freshly drawn
  water (from a kettle)
milk
sugar
lemon (if you must)
Cup and saucer per
  person

Serves 2

For all those in search of a little extramarital activity, a tea bar on a train station platform might not be the first place you'd contemplate visiting. However, you just never know where you might find that elusive man with a clean hankie in his pocket if you look hard enough. Despite the frustrations of being unable to say goodbye properly, Laura and Alec still managed to get the chance for a nice sit down and a decent cup of tea. And as we all know, those two things go beautifully together! Just like Laura and Alec, in fact.

[VOICE-OVER]

Loose leaf tea is the only way to make a really good cup of tea. The leaves are larger, can move around the pot better and infuse beautifully. If you insist on using a tea bag in a mug not only are you a Philistine but you will not get a decent cup of tea and should consider drinking instant coffee instead.

[MISE-EN-SCENE]

1. Empty the kettle of any old water. Don't put it down the sink, use it to water the house plants or fill up the iron.

2. Fill the kettle with fresh water from the tap and put the kettle on to boil.

3. Empty the teapot. Any cold tea can be kept to soak raisins in for a nice fruit cake if you have the coupons. Tea leaves can either go on your compost heap or around the roses. Rinse the pot out well.

4. Once the kettle has boiled pour a small amount of boiling water into the pot and swill this around. This will warm the pot. Tip this water away.

5. Spoon one heaped teaspoon of leaf tea per person into the pot. Add a final spoon of tea for the pot. Top up with boiling water. Stir the pot once and put the lid on.

6. Cover the pot with a tea cosy and leave to brew for at least 5 minutes.

7. Now for the big debate, milk first or tea first? I put the milk in first.

8. Using a tea strainer, pour a nice cup of tea. Before the war a slice of cake would be on offer. You'd be hard pressed to share a digestive now.

9. The youngest member of the family is now delegated to refill everyone's cups and do the washing up when tea is over.

Gibson

ALL ABOUT EVE (1950)

'I'll admit I may have seen better days, but I'm still not to be had for the price of a cocktail like a salted peanut'

[CAST & CREW]

crushed ice
50ml (2fl oz) gin
25ml (1fl oz) vermouth
1 or 2 cocktail onions,
  plus a few drops of the
  onion juice from the
  jar

Serves 1

Margo Channing's jealousy of those whose careers are in the ascendancy while hers is waning, eats away at her throughout the film.

The more green-eyed she becomes, the more waspish her comments are. Her consumption of these spiteful little drinks doesn't help her mood much either. Before the party gets into full swing, Margo asks for a very dry martini, while suggesting that her younger rival, Eve, should have a milkshake. What she gets is a Gibson. Then another, and another and another, all downed with her natural timidity.

'Fasten your seatbelts, it's going to be a bumpy night!'

[VOICE-OVER]

Domestic gins made in the USA are sometimes seen as soft gins, perhaps with a slightly lower ABV and with less complex botanicals. The imported, or harder gins, are often stronger and have a greater depth of flavour. The number of cocktails Margo downs, and the speed with which she does it, probably shows why she ordered a domestic rather than an imported gin. That, possibly, and the opportunity to comment on the domesticity of her guests in her usual frank style.

[MISE-EN-SCENE]

1. Place ice in a mixing glass.

2. Pour the gin and the vermouth over the ice. (The less vermouth you use the drier the drink becomes. Winston Churchill famously liked his martinis so dry he simply left the open bottle of vermouth next to the poured gin.)

3. Shake or stir as is your preference and strain into a martini glass.

4. Plop in one or two cocktail onions. If you want a slightly smoother drink, add a few drops of the onion juice.

5. Knock back several of these but try to keep those waspish comments in check. You may well live to regret it in the morning and have a serious hangover to boot.

Pan Galactic Gargleblaster

THE HITCHHIKER'S GUIDE TO THE GALAXY (2005)

'A cup of tea would restore my normality'

[CAST & CREW]

1 measure of vodka (the juice from a bottle of ol'janx spirit)
1 measure clam juice (water from the seas of Santraginus V)
1 measure ice cold gin (3 cubes of Arcturan Mega-gin)
Tonic water with lime (4 litres of Fallian marsh gas to bubble through it)
1 measure mint syrup (Over the back of a silver spoon float a measure of Qalactin Hypermint extract)
1 Tic Tac (tooth of an Algolian Suntiger)
lime peel (Sprinkle Zamphuor)
olive
Serves 1

There have been days when, on the advice of a travel guide, I've woken up with a hangover that made me feel as if I had two heads like Zaphod Beeblebrox – seemingly the only alien able to consume three Pan Galactic Gargleblaster's and live to tell the tale.

This infamous space cocktail is one of the most beloved elements of Douglas Adams' timeless and surreal cosmic adventure. Indeed, many internet sites are devoted as to how to perfectly recreate this mind-bending, head-bludgeoner down on Earth.

Well, this is my take on Douglas Adams' classic recipe and should look just like it too.

[VOICE-OVER]

As Ford Prefect advises, it is always best to travel through space clinging to a towel. I suggest you do the same if you wish to drink a Pan Galactic Gargleblaster, you know, just in case.

[SERVING SUGGESTION]

Before you sink this drink, remember Marvin the Paranoid Android's advice, 'I've calculated your chance of survival, but I don't think you'll like it.'

[MISE-EN-SCENE]

1. Take a cocktail shaker and fill with ice.

2. Add in the vodka, gin, clam juice and mint syrup. Shake well and strain into a tall glass.

3. Top up with the lime tonic water.

4. Take the lime peel and twist it over the top of the glass to release the lime oils onto the surface of the cocktail.

5. Drop the lime peel into the drink. Add the olive and the tic tac.

6. Place two straws into the drink, one for each mouth.

7. Drink ... but ... very ... carefully

Martini

GOLDFINGER (1964)

'Shaken, not stirred'

[CAST & CREW]

Ice
75ml (3fl oz) Gordon's
  gin
25ml (1fl oz) vodka
15ml ($^1/_2$ fl oz) Kina
  Lillet
a thin slice of lemon
  peel

Serves 1

In Movieland, everyone's favourite Bond, Sean Connery, was the first to utter the classic line 'shaken, not stirred' in *Goldfinger*. Since then it has become one of the most quoted lines in movie history – especially when coupled with a thick Scottish accent.

In Daniel Craig's thrilling re-boot of *Casino Royale,* our hero Bond gives the audience the exact recipe of Ian Fleming's favourite tipple and by doing so also suggests the origins behind why this particular drink is his weapon of choice. Bond even goes so far as to give this saucy little number a name, Vesper, after his one and only true love, Vesper Lynd, the woman who will eventually betray him.

It is Bond's classic martini above all else that he is most associated with. Though to be fair, he likes his fair share of top-quality champagne too!

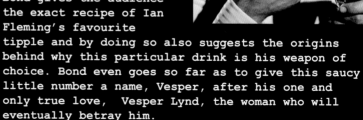

[VOICE-OVER]

To drink the original Vesper Martini as Ian Fleming would appreciate you will need Kina Lillet. This can be hard to find though vermouth makes a good substitute. However, the Kina Lillet gives a faint golden tinge that won't be present if you use vermouth. Kina Lillet is French so try and source this on your next booze cruise if you crave such authenticity. Local shops rather than l'hypermarché might be your best hunting ground for this elusive liqueur.

[MISE-EN-SCENE]

1. Put on your posh frock or your black tie and invite any international villains you happen to know over to play poker in your living room.

2. Place ice in a mixing glass.

3. Pour the Gordon's, vodka and the Kina Lillet over the ice.

4. Shake.

5. Pour into a martini glass and add a thin slither of lemon peel. Give the peel a little twist as you add it to release the lemon oils into the glass.

6. Repeat as necessary throughout the evening until the world as we know it is saved from the forces of evil.

'Hey, careful, man, there's a beverage here!'

[CAST & CREW]

50ml (15fl oz) vodka
50ml (15fl oz) coffee
 liqueur
25ml (7fl oz) single
 cream
ice

Serves 1 (enough to last
 you the entire film!)

When The Dude has his identity accidentally muddled
with that of The Big Lebowski, his laid-back attitude
to life becomes threatened.

As The Dude's life collides again and again with
the world of Bunny and Maude Lebowski it gets even
more bizarre. Missing toes and rugs, the death of
Donny, the appearance of The Stranger, and not to
mention those weird, unsettling, acid flashbacks.

While the number of joints and White Russians that
The Dude pushes through his system don't help his
overall sense of confusion, eventually 'the Dude
abides' and solves the riddle ... and gets a new rug.

[VOICE-OVER]

Should you wish to take the Big Lebowski challenge and match The Dude drink for drink whilst watching this movie, not only are you likely to pass out before the end of the film, you are possibly never going to wake up again. If, however, you'd like to make a batch of White Russians to share with friends then this is the exact quantity drunk in the film.

[MISE-EN-SCENE]

1. Put down the joint and try to focus for a moment. Find a suitable and hopefully clean glass.

2. Add a handful of ice to this short tumbler.

3. Pour in the vodka and give a little stir. A swizzle stick is best but a cleanish finger will do.

4. Now add in the coffee liqueur and stir again.

5. Top up with the cream. Lie back on a comfortable, unblemished rug. Enjoy.

6. 'Refill?'

7. 'Does the Pope shit in the woods?'

'I am the last barman poet, I see America drinking the fabulous cktails I make, Americans getting stinky on something I stir or shake'

[CAST & CREW]

shot of vodka
shot of creme de cacao
shot of single cream

rves 1

Cocktails and dreams is the motto of this fabulously 80s movie.

Personally, I was never one for short creamy cocktails such as the Velvet Hammer, especially if you happen to reside on the Carribean shores like Brian and Doug. Light, fruity cocktails like Rum Punch's and Tequila Sunrises are much more thirst-quenching! If you do enjoy the shorter cocktail (and no that isn't a covert reference to Tom Cruise) try one of these Velvet Hammers next time you watch the movie.

[VOICE-OVER]

The list of cocktails rapped to the audience by Tom Cruise in the movie:

1. *Sex on the Beach*
2. *Schnapps made from peach*
3. *Velvet Hammer*
4. *Alabama Slammer*
5. *Things with juice and froth*
6. *Pink Squirrel*
7. *Three-toed Sloth*
8. *Iced Tea*
9. *Kamakazi*
10. *Orgasm*
11. *Death Spasm*
12. *Singapore Sling*
13. *Dingaling*

[MISE-EN-SCENE]

1. Flirt heavily with the customers.

2. Fill the shaker up with ice.

3. Showboat with the bottles.

4. Pour in the vodka, creme de cacao and the cream. Shake well.

5. Showboat with the cocktail shaker.

6. Strain into a chilled martini glass.

7. Should we let it breathe?

8. It hasn't breathed for fifty years, it's dead. Let's just drink it.

A Selection of Wine

SIDEWAYS (2004)

'Quaffable, but uh... far from transcendent'

[CAST & CREW]

One bottle of each:

Californian Pinot Noir
Champagne
Pinot Noir Vin Gris
Syrah
Chardonnay
Cabernet Franc
Sauvignon Blanc
Merlot(or not, if you
  are like Miles!)

Serves (however many
  guests you have!)

Also required:

Corkscrew
Glasses
Fridge

The *Sideway*'s effect on the sales of Pinot Noir lasted for some time after the movie came out. Thankfully it didn't have a devastating effect on the much maligned Merlot as I rather enjoy a glass or several of that particular grape. This brilliantly observed movie shows how being an oenophile is now an accepted way of life. Some of the 'other' proclivities of both Jack and Miles may take a little more understanding however, especially from friends, family and, ahem, fiancées.

[VOICE-OVER]

I tend to buy wine by the region rather than use the grape variety as a factor. There are many reasons for this: I know I enjoy a particular style of wine and this can be found in these areas. Also the variety name changes from region to region and just completely confuses me. One very good reason for going to a wine tasting when they are offered in store, as well as free wine, is that you may learn something new. Just stay sober enough to remember it.

[MISE-EN-SCENE]

1. Ensure the wine is at the correct temperature for serving.

2. Place wine glass in front of each guest.

3. Uncork, or more likely unscrew the lid of your bottle of wine. Pour each person a third to a half glass of wine.

4. Unless you are on a mission to see who gets drunk quickest please also have glasses of water available for your guests.

5. Discuss the merits of each wine.

6. Repeat with a different wine.

7. Resist the temptation to play Twister or send emails whilst under the influence of either the Pinot or the Chardonnay and heaven forbid you should even consider Merlot.

Movie Drinks

Watching *Sideways* makes me yearn for a decent Pinot Noir, and I always get the taste for mulled wine whenever I watch *It's A Wonderful Life*. Watching these movies make me want to get into the spirit of things too and, of course, enjoy the same fancy cocktails, or tipples, that are up on the big screen.

Here are some more of my favourite movies with their accompanying drinks. If you drink as you watch one thing's for certain – it'll make the film experience unforgettable!

The Blues Brothers
(1978) –
Night Train Express
Wine (17.5%!)

Casablanca (1942) –
Veuve Cliquot '26

An Affair to Remember
(1957) –
Pink Champagne

It's a Wonderful Life
(1946) –
Mulled Wine

The Maltese Falcon
(1941) –
A Mickey Finn Special

The Silence of the Lambs
(1991) –
Chianti

Withnail and I (1986) –
In order of the film:
$9\frac{1}{2}$ glasses of red wine
1 pint of cider
1 shot of lighter fluid
$2\frac{1}{2}$ shots of gin
6 glasses of sherry
13 whiskys
$\frac{1}{2}$ a pint of ale

Arsenic and Old Lace
(1944) –
Elderberry Wine
1 tbsp of Arsenic
$\frac{1}{2}$ tsp strychnine
A pinch of cyanide

The Big Sleep (1946) –
Brandy

Notorious (1946) –
Ler Cru Burgundy,
Volnay Cailleret
Bouchard

Every Day's a Holiday (1930)–
Bellini

Top Hat (1935) –
A Horse's Neck
4 parts whisky
Ginger ale
3 dashes angostura
bitters

Dark Victory (1939) –
Pink Gin

James Bond (1953-present) –
Dom Perignon '53
(not a '55!)

Anna Christie (1930) –
Whiskey
Ginger ale on the side

The Nutty Professor (1963) –
The Alaskan Polar Bear
Heater
Two shots of vodka
A little rum
Some bitter
Vinegar
A shot of vermouth
A shot of gin
Brandy
Lemon peel
Orange peel
Cherry
Some more scotch

Arthur (1981) –
Scotch (on the rocks!)

El Dorado (1966) –
Whisky

Cat on a Hot Tin Roof (1958) –
Bourbon

Leaving Las Vegas (1995) –
Vodka
Whisky (bourbon and
Scotch)
Gin
Beer
Tequila

The Philadelphia Story (1940) –
Sherry
Martini's (gin and
vermouth)

Raiders of the Lost Ark (1981) –
Marian's Whisky
Belloq's family label
liquor

A Streetcar Named Desire (1951) –
Scotch
'Southern Cheer'liqueur

The Hangover (2009) –
Jagermeister

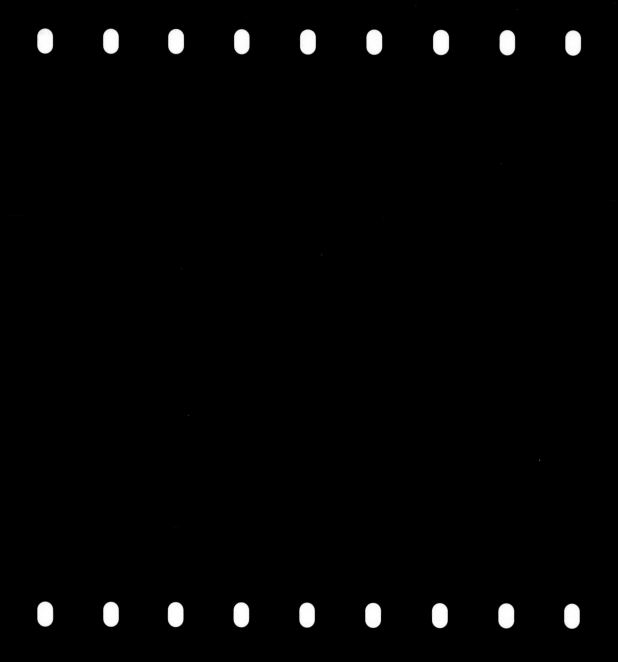

Shorts

Small, simple and satisfying.
A great place to start...

Bantha Milkshake

STAR WARS: EPISODE IV A NEW HOPE (1977)

'Luke's not a farmer, Owen. He has too much of his father in him'

[CAST & CREW]

150g (6oz) blueberries
500g (1lb 2oz) blueberry
  or natural yogurt
honey, to taste
2 tbsp porridge oats
1 tsp ginger, grated
a splash of milk

Serves 1

The *Star Wars* universe is a strange, yet oddly familiar, place. You would have thought that in such a sophisticated society, surrounded by spaceships and droids, Luke's plastic milkshake cup and spoon would have been more advanced. But alas, no!

I've made this Bantha shake with blueberries to match the colour of the milk you see in Uncle Owen's cave-house on Tatooine.

This is the perfect snack to make for your kids when you watch the *Star Wars* films *every* Christmas time or even a fun treat for you and your friends next time you suggest watching all six episodes back to back on a Sunday afternoon.

[VOICE-OVER]

This basic smoothie recipe can be adapted to include a whole variety of berry fruits. The ginger gives a back-of-the-tongue tingle to the berries, black pepper works well with strawberries, and mint goes very well with apple. Kiwi smoothies taste great but if you feed them to small boys they will comment on the smoothies' resemblance to snot. Be warned.

[MISE-EN-SCENE]

1. Rinse the blueberries, taste one and pop the rest into a blender.

2. Add the yogurt. If the blueberries were a little tart, now is the time to add honey to taste.

3. Add the oats and stir well. Put the grated ginger into the milkshake.

4. Blend until smooth, then thin the smoothie with milk until it reaches the desired consistency. (I have no idea of the consistency of Bantha milk, so let's guess at double cream.)

5. Pour into a plastic tumbler (or half-pint glass) and add a couple of thick straws.

6. Resist the temptation to discuss light sabres or the legacy left to you by your father while drinking - it may cause a variance in the force.

Blue Soup

BRIDGET JONES' DIARY (2001)

'We have blue soup to start, orange pudding to end, and, well, for a main course you have, uh, congealed green gunge'

[CAST & CREW]

350g (12oz) leek whites, finely sliced (save the green tops for another dish)
150g (5oz) onion, finely chopped
250g (9oz) blue potatoes, finely chopped (salad blue is a good variety to use)
large knob of butter
1 glass white wine (Chardonnay, if you must)
2 wine glasses chicken or vegetable stock or water
300ml (½ pint) milk
salt and white pepper
blue food colouring and a few cooked noodles, to serve (optional)

Serves 4

Ever so befuddlingly handsome and charming Mark Darcy starts by describing Bridget Jones as a 'verbally incontinent spinster who drinks like a fish, smokes like a chimney and dresses like her mother'. But what he has yet to discover is that her cooking skills are beyond terrible as well.

So take a stand people, swerve to avoid the bland turkey curry buffet, get into the kitchen and start cooking this recipe for Bridget's Blue Soup. As Mr Darcy so rightly points out, 'Blue is good. If you ask me there isn't enough blue food.'

[VOICE-OVER]

Only ever cook with wine you are prepared to drink. Anything that makes your nose wrinkle when drunk will do the same when added to food. This is especially true of food you serve to guests.

[MISE-EN-SCENE]

1. Melt the butter in a large lidded pan and add in the vegetables. Cover and fry gently for 5 minutes to soften.

2. Tip in the wine and cook for 5 minutes. (This will allow the alcohol to burn off and therefore doesn't count towards Bridget's tally in her diary.) Add the stock or water and cook for 20 minutes, or until the potatoes begin to break down and become mushy.

3. Add the milk and stir to combine. Cool slightly, then blend using a stick blender. (If you want to use a liquidiser, remember that hot soup in a blender can lead to a huge mess on the kitchen walls, floors and ceiling, and possibly second-degree burns. You have been warned!)

4. If the soup isn't blue enough, add a little food colouring. If you want to be even more authentic add a few strands of cooked noodles to replicate the string that caused Bridget's culinary oddity.

5. Count your blessings, this won't take four hours to cook nor will it give you a bottom the size of Brazil. Now, in the words of Bridget herself, bugger off...

Now, I wouldn't follow Luke's grandstanding and eat 50 hard-boiled eggs as a way to raise either your profile, your self-esteem or your cool-ness. The only thing likely to become elevated is your cholesterol level. What a great scene though...

Raw Egg Smoothie

ROCKY (1976)

'I feel like a Kentucky Fried idiot'

[CAST & CREW] Half a dozen eggs

Filling a pint glass with raw eggs and then chugging them down was as close as Stallone's aspiring boxer could get to a protein shake. Under no circumstances should anyone who is very young (babies to toddlers), elderly, pregnant or already unwell eat raw eggs. Actually, I wouldn't recommend this to anyone who has a strong gag reflex either!

[VOICE-OVER]

If you have space in your kitchen, eggs are best kept out of the fridge. They produce far better results in baking when used at room temperature. It goes without saying that a cold egg will take longer to come to the boil than a warm one.

[MISE-EN-SCENE]

1. Place the egg gently into a pan.

2. Pour over cold water to cover the egg completely.

3. Place the pan over a medium heat and bring to the boil. As soon as the water boils start timing. Four minutes will give you a soft-boiled egg ready for dipping but to recreate this scene then you will need 7 to 8 minutes for a hard-boiled egg.

4. Plunge the hard-boiled egg into ice cold water to stop the cooking process.

5. Get counting, 1,2,3...25,26,27... 48,49,50!

- -

[VOICE-OVER]

If you grow tired of common or garden chicken eggs then why not replace them with ova of another sort:

Quail
Gull
Turkey
Duck
Goose
Ostrich

[MISE-EN-SCENE]

1. Break the eggs gently into a large glass

2. Down them in one.

3. Resist the very strong urge to throw up!

Crab Dumplings

EAT DRINK MAN WOMAN (1994)

'Raising daughters is like cooking a meal. You lose your appetite by the time you're finished'

[CAST & CREW]

1 tsp cornflour
squeeze of lime juice,
  plus extra to serve
1 tsp soy sauce, plus
  extra to serve
1cm ($\frac{1}{2}$ in) ginger,
  peeled and grated
1 garlic clove, grated
$\frac{1}{2}$ tsp caster sugar
salt
50g (2oz) cooked prawns
60g (2 $\frac{1}{4}$ oz) white crab
  meat
3 water chestnuts,
  chopped
1 spring onion, finely
  chopped
12 wonton wrappers
sesame oil

Makes 12

I would happily watch the opening sequence of this magnificent Ang Lee movie over and over again. It is a film that makes us all look again at what our priorities are and what perhaps they ought to be instead. In a time before 'gastroporn' was readily available on every television channel, *Eat Drink Man Woman* was one of the few places us members of the grubby-apron brigade could get our filthy kicks.

Chef Chu creates his banquets as a way of expressing his love for his family. Family meals in the movie are, as in real life, fraught with hidden meaning, where much is shared – but much is also kept secret.

[VOICE-OVER]

To make a crispy treat try frying these wontons instead of steaming. Cook for 3-4 minutes in hot oil until golden brown and crispy. Fried dumplings are blisteringly hot so leave to cool for a moment before eating.

[SERVING SUGGESTION]

If you want to vary the proportion of the crab and prawns then do, but try to keep the overall quantity of mixture the same. Chilli makes a good addition too.

[MISE-EN-SCENE]

1. Put the cornflour, lime juice, soy sauce, ginger and garlic into a bowl and mix together. Stir in the sugar and salt to taste. Add more lime juice if needed.

2. Finely chop the prawns to mince. Add to the lime mixture with the crabmeat, water chestnuts and spring onions. Mix well and leave to infuse for 5 minutes.

3. Take a wonton wrapper. Brush the edges with water. Place a teaspoonful of the mixture into the middle of the wrapper. Draw the edges together to make a money bag. Make sure the edges are well sealed.

4. Place the dumplings in a bamboo steamer on a plate lightly oiled with sesame oil and steam for about 10 minutes. Serve with a little lime and soy mixed together as a dip.

Fish Ceviche

A FISH CALLED WANDA (1988)

'Wake up, Limey fish!'

[CAST & CREW]

250g (9oz) firm white
  fish (sea bass, halibut
  or even tuna), boned
  and skinned
juice of 3 limes
juice of 1 lemon
2 shallots, finely
  chopped
3 sticks celery, finely
  chopped
fennel, finely sliced
  (optional)
chilli, finely chopped
  (optional)

To serve:
spring onion, finely
  shredded
coriander
tortilla chips
green salad (optional)

Serves 4 as a starter

Having shared his chips in a unique fashion with the s-s-s-stuttering Ken, over-the-top Otto then turns his evil attention to the still-swimming fish in Ken's exotic fish tank to accompany his remaining chips. Deciding to cruelly eat the fish in their natural state Otto works his way through the entire tank one-by-one. Wanda, Ken's most beloved Angel fish, is saved until very last but, sadly, can't escape the inevitable.
  Come on, Wanda – gullet time!

[VOICE-OVER]

If slicing fish is too much of a palaver then chop the fish into small dice, stir in the shallots, celery, juice and chilli and refrigerate. Continue the recipe as shown but serve in a big bowl with tortilla chips to scoop up this fishy loveliness. Mexican beer is best with this version.

[VARIATION]

Make this recipe your own. Add in or take away ingredients you don't like, except the fish bit of course. Find a fish you like, tweak the added extras and enjoy this simple dish. Please eat it out of sight of any fish tanks.

[MISE—EN—SCENE]

1. Cut the fish across the grain into even slices no more than 1cm thick.

2. Place the fish in a non-metallic bowl and cover with the lemon and lime juice, shallots and celery. If you are choosing to use fennel or chilli then add this too now.

3. Leave covered in the fridge for 20-30 minutes until opaque. (Do not leave longer than this because the citrus will cause the fish to break down too much giving it a rather unpleasant, mushy texture.)

4. Place on a serving dish and sprinkle with spring onions, coriander and perhaps a little more chilli. The addition of a green salad would be a good idea too. Squeeze over a little more citrus. If you really fancy some chips you can have those too - but please, no ketchup!

French Toast

KRAMER VS KRAMER (1979)

'French toast you want, French toast you got'

[CAST & CREW]

1 tbsp flour
2 large eggs
125ml (4fl oz) milk
1 tbsp sugar
pinch of salt
pinch of cinnamon
splash of vanilla
  extract
butter, for frying
oil, for frying
4-6 slices white bread

Serves 2

Never before have I seen a man who looks so ill at ease in an apron! Ted's disastrous cooking episode with Billy could have had me in hysterics, but the overall feeling instead was of huge sadness for both characters as they were unable to bond properly with one another as father and son.

One lesson we all learned from watching Ted's first attempt at French toast was never touch the hot handle of a cast iron frying pan, unless you want to expand your child's vocabulary with an excellent example of how to use the F-word in context.

As for French toast itself – delicious – everybody

[VOICE-OVER]

Serve with warm maple syrup, bacon, fruit compôte or blueberries. Try not to add a side order of expletives and venom à la Ted Kramer.

[MISE-EN-SCENE]

1. Put the flour and eggs in a large bowl or flat dish (not a coffee mug). Whisk together until well combined and frothy.

2. Pour in the milk, sugar, salt, cinnamon and vanilla and whisk again.

3. Heat a large frying pan and add a knob of butter and a splash of oil.

4. Dip a slice of bread into the batter to coat both sides, but don't let it soak the batter up like a sponge. Allow any excess batter to drip back into the bowl.

5. Lay the bread in the pan and cook for 2-3 minutes until brown and crispy underneath. You need to be vigilant. Do not allow small children to distract you at this point or you will have to start again. Turn the bread over and cook until golden and crispy.

6. Cut the French toast into half on the diagonal and serve.

7. Repeat with the next slice of bread. After a while you should have a good production line going. Please have a cloth ready to wrap around the pan handle just in case you want to move it as this will save you both from saying rude words and third-degree burns.

Small Bread Sandwiches

SPINAL TAP (1984)

'You'd like bigger bread?

[CAST & CREW]

A selection of breads of
  small diameter (length
  is not an issue but
  girth matters)

**For the sandwich
filling:**
6 luncheon meat slices
6 processed cheese
  slices

Serves 4-6

Having struggled for half an hour to fold the bread
around the filling, bewildered Nigel Tufnell gives up
and releases his inner diva - turning it up to eleven
as he does so. In one of modern movies most popular
comedic scenes, the backstage meat and the cheese
slices on offer for Spinal Tap are regular sized, but
the bread, however, is just much too small and thinly
sliced. The ensuing conversation between Nigel
and manager Ian as to how to solve this problem is
a wonderfully funny interplay - the sandwiches
serving as a thinly sliced metaphor for the growing
frustrations within the band.

[VOICE-OVER]

It is far better to use two slices of buttered bread to hold your filling than try to encase the middle of your sandwich with one folded slice. Whatever its size the bread may well break and, given rock star tendencies, so could you.

[QUOTE]

NIGEL: No no no no, look - look this - this miniature bread, it's like, I've been working with this for about a half an hour now - I can't figure out ...You've got this -

IAN: You'd like bigger bread?

NIGEL: Exactly! I don't understand how...

IAN: You could just fold it though...

NIGEL: Well no, then it's half the size.

[MISE-EN-SCENE]

1. Slice the bread thinly and butter on one side. Lay the buttered bread on a serving platter.

2. Take the slices of luncheon meat and cheese. Spend a little time deciding how best to fold the filling to fit the bread. Do not fold the bread as it will break.

3. If the above instructions take more than thirty minutes to work out you may be a closet heavy metal band member.

4. Put the whole lot back on the serving platter and either pop out to the sandwich shop for a tuna and sweetcorn on brown or, better still, send out a minion to get one for you.

Turkey Sandwich

WHEN HARRY MET SALLY (1989)

'I'll have what she's having'

[CAST & CREW]

2 thick slices fresh
   white bread
butter, for spreading
mayonnaise, for
   spreading
lettuce, shredded, for
   topping
cucumber, sliced, for
   topping
tomato, sliced, for
   topping
100g (3 ½ oz) sliced
   roast turkey breast
salt and ground black
   pepper

Serves 1

When Harry and Sally decide to have a light snack in a New York deli – over discussions of each other's sex lives – Sally's turkey sandwich gives rise to the most fantastically vocal orgasm ever performed in (a Hollywood) film. As Sally's groans and moans fill the room and attract the attention of the other diners, Harry becomes more and more uncomfortable. It's a terrific scene for women and foodies alike!

Whether my turkey sandwich recipe triggers the same response that Sally experienced may depend on who you are with when you eat it, but rest assured, this is one tasty turkey sandwich regardless.

[VOICE-OVER]

The matching sandwich that Harry ordered was pastrami on rye bread. To make one, follow instructions as above but omit the mayonnaise and add mustard instead. A side order of dill pickles is a fine accompaniment. This sandwich has no known side effects, except indigestion if eaten too quickly.

[MISE-EN-SCENE]

1. Place the bread on a large plate. Spread one slice with butter and generously slather the other with mayonnaise.

2. Cover one slice with shredded lettuce, cucumber and tomatoes. This will give the eater something to pick out if they are incredibly fussy.

3. Fill the sandwich with huge quantities of turkey (wafer-thin works really well in this case but if you prefer the thicker-cut turkey then that's fine too. Season.

4. Press the second slice of bread on top. Slice the sandwich in two. Impale each half with a frilled cocktail stick to hold it all together.

5. Take a bite and see what happens. If there are no tingles at all then fake it. Go on, you know you can!

Chilli Cheese Dog

DRAGNET (1987)

'Let me tell you something Mister, unlike you, outside of cigarettes I only have one vice, and a good chilli dog is it'

[CAST & CREW]

500g (1lb 2oz) minced beef
1 finely chopped onion
2 finely chopped cloves of garlic
1 freshly chopped chilli - jalapeno, red chilli or bird's-eye, you choose the heat.
1 tbsp vegetable oil
500g (1lb 2oz) box of passata
water if needed
1 tsp smoked paprika
8 hot dog buns
8 hot dogs or frankfurters
250g (9oz) strong cheese, grated
ketchup and mustard

Serves 4

In between solving a ridiculous P.A.G.A.N. crime and bickering constantly with one another, Detectives Joe Friday and Pep Streebeck stop off at Pink's restaurant in Los Angeles to let Joe indulge in his chilli dog habit. 'You know the kinds of things that can fall into an industrial sausage press? Not excluding the rodent hairs and bug excrement?' Pep Streebeck offers.'I hate you,' Friday replies.

Pink's Restaurant exists in real life and is a popular celebrity hang out where the chilli dogs are often publicly declared as the best in the world. Certainly, Joe Friday would agree.

[VOICE OVER]

This chilli should be spoonable but not overly runny or lumpy. The order you place the chilli, cheese and hot dog in the bun is up to you. If you prefer sliced processed cheese or even that squeezy cheese then fine.

[MISE-EN-SCENE]

1. Finely chop the onion and garlic. Heat a little oil in a pan and sauté the onion and garlic until translucent.

2. Place the minced beef into the pan and break up any large lumps with a wooden spoon. Cook the mince until the meat has browned. Stir in the paprika and the chopped chilli at this point. Cook out for a minute or so until the chilli has softened a little.

3. Pour in the passata and allow the mince mixture to come up to a simmer. Reduce the heat and leave the chilli to barely simmer for at least half an hour. You can leave this for several hours if you need to. If the mixture thickens too much just add a little water to thin it back to a spooning consistency.

4. Heat a large frying pan or a griddle. Whilst this is heating boil your frankfurters according to the pack instructions. Once cooked sear the hot dog briefly on the pan or griddle to give a slightly smoky and charred flavour. Split your hot dog buns. Use this same pan to toast your buns if you wish.

5. Build that dog. Open the bun, lay in your sausage. Top with chilli and the grated cheese. Optional extras are mustard and ketchup.

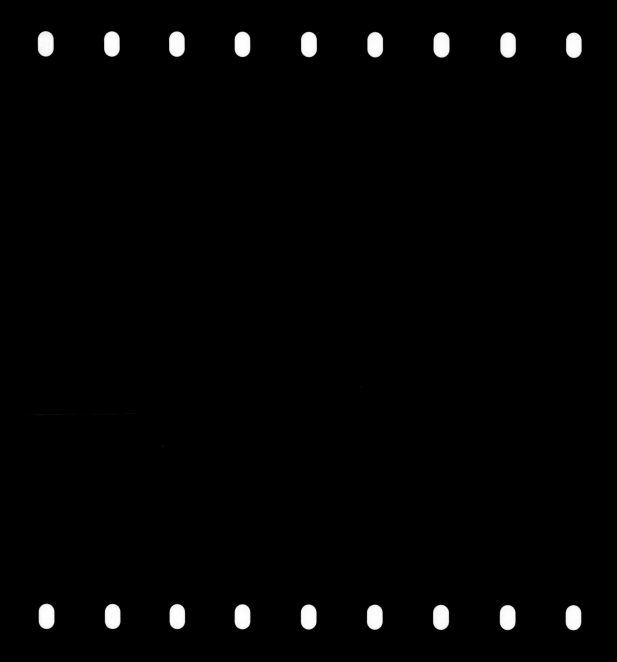

Main Feature

It's time for the main attraction.
Set tastebuds to stun...

Big Kahuna Burger

PULP FICTION (1994)

'Hamburgers. The cornerstone of any nutritious breakfast'

[CAST & CREW]

oil, for frying
1 onion, finely chopped
1 garlic clove, finely
  chopped
500g (1lb 2oz) minced
  beef
4 burger buns
4 cheese slices
  (optional)
salt and ground black
  pepper
mayonnaise, tomato
  ketchup, pickles,
  lettuce and French
  fries, to serve
  (optional)

Serves 4

'Mmm-mmmm, that is a tasty burger' hitman Jules begins moments before opening fire on a couple of petrified double-crossers. And he's right – from the look of it it sure does look tasty.

In possibly one of cinema's most famous foodie scenes, Jules extolls the virtues of a Big Kahuna Burger – Quentin Tarantino's real life burger joint – before taking a bite big enough to make the entire audience salivate. Altogether now...

'...and I will strike down upon thee with great vengeance and furious anger those who would attempt to poison and destroy my brothers...'

[VOICE-OVER]

You can replace the beef mince with lamb or pork if you prefer. Lamb with cumin and a minty yogurt sauce would be tasty. The pork would go well with the pineapple to make Big Kahuna Burgers. Turkey mince is fine too but add a little oil as the leanness of the turkey may cause the patty to be a little dry.

[MISE-EN-SCENE]

1. Heat a little oil in a pan and sauté the onion and garlic for 5 minutes until translucent. Allow to cool. (Cooking the onion and garlic will prevent the post-burger breath that might just antagonise Jules even further.)

2. Place the minced beef in a large bowl and break up with a fork. Tip in the cooled onions and garlic and season well.

3. Use your hands to combine the mixture thoroughly, then divide into four equal portions. Shape the meat into patties and pop in the fridge for 30 minutes to firm up before cooking.

4. Using a griddle pan or the barbecue, cook the burgers for 3-4 minutes on each side until no longer pink in the middle. Lightly toast the buns.

5. Place each burger on a half bun. To make a Hamburger Royale, top with a slice of cheese. To make Le Big Mac, add the sauces, pickles and lettuce. If you wish to be fully metric, then take a rain check on the ketchup and drown your French fries in mayonnaise.

Cannoli

THE GODFATHER (1972)

'Leave the gun, take the cannoli'

[CAST & CREW]

275g (10oz) plain flour
1 tsp baking powder
1 tbsp granulated sugar
pinch of salt
$^1/_2$ tsp cinnamon
25g (1oz) butter
1 egg
75ml (2$^1/_2$ fl oz) marsala
  (but any wine will do!)
vegetable oil, for
  frying
water or egg whites, to
  seal
icing sugar, to dust

Makes 30 strips of dough

Family comes first in the Corleone's household. But food runs a close second.

Having decided to remove Paulie from the family 'permanently', Sonny takes him on a short drive into the countryside. It will be the last journey he ever takes.

Making the journey too was a box of cannoli — tubes of cinnamon-tinged pastry waiting to be filled with creamy ricotta — an utterly mouth-watering Italian meal.

Marlon Brando, later on in his life, was reported to have enjoyed whole sandwiches consisting of just a pound of cooked bacon shoved into an entire loaf of bread. Not as tasty as cannoli — but certainly not an offer you could refuse!

[VOICE-OVER]

Cannoli tubes are widely available in the US or online but you can also make cannoli. Cut the dough into 2cm (3/4in) wide strips and fry until golden. Dust with icing sugar or dip in chocolate to serve. To fill cannoli tubes you need a tub of ricotta, sweetened to taste with icing sugar. Stir in chopped chocolate, pistachios, candied fruits or grated lemon peel, then pipe the mixture into the tubes. Dust with icing sugar and serve. (It's easy to see why Clemenza wanted to take the cannoli and leave the gun.)

[MISE-EN-SCENE]

1. Sift the flour, baking powder, sugar, salt and cinnamon into a large bowl or directly on to the work surface, as if you were making pasta.

2. Rub in the butter until the mixture resembles bread crumbs. Make a well in the centre and add the egg and the wine. Using a fork, or even better your fingers, work the wet ingredients into the dry. Stir the mixture from the centre outwards, drawing in the dry ingredients as you go.

3. When well combined knead the dough for 5-10 minutes until it becomes smooth and elastic in texture. If the mix is a little dry, add a splash more wine; if too sticky, add more flour.

4. Place back in the bowl, cover with clear film and leave to relax in a warm place for 30 minutes.

5. Roll out the dough thinly to about 2mm (1 1/2in) thick. Cut out rounds with a diameter of 5cm (2in) to wrap around cannoli tubes. Seal with a dab of water or egg white.

6. Put the oil on to heat. To deep-fry, heat the oil to 190℃. If shallow-frying, use 2 tbsp oil at a medium-high heat. Lower the tubes into the oil and fry until golden. Remove from the oil and allow to drain and cool on kitchen paper.

7. Dust with icing sugar or dip in melted chocolate to serve.

1 cooked lobster
splash of white wine
  (optional)

For the sauce:
1 lemon, zested and
  juiced
125g (4oz) unsalted
  butter (if you have
  salted, be careful when
  you season), diced
1 tbsp fresh parsley,
  finely chopped
salt and ground black
  pepper

**Serves 2 — Lobster is an
aphrodisiac after all!**

Whilst Alvy and Annie may have imagined that cooking lobster for supper would be a romantic meal, the reality of cooking the lobster leaves them both incapacitated with laughter and incapable of sending one lobster on its final journey.

After Alvy suggests calling 911 and asking for the lobster squad and reminding Annie that she 'speaks shellfish' Alvy comes up with a magnificent solution to this crustacean crisis: 'Maybe if I put a little dish of butter sauce here with a nutcracker, it will run out the other side.'

[VOICE-OVER]

Although the whole scene is jam-packed full of fun and there is a real sexual frisson in the air, I'd give the fresh lobster-chasing a miss and stick to buying ready-cooked instead. Save your energy for after the meal. Well, you know what they say about shellfish!

[VARIATION]

If you really want to cook the lobster yourself – perhaps you live by the sea or are particularly brave – then this is how to do it. Place the lobster in the freezer for at least 2 hours to send it into a coma-like state and allowing you to kill it humanely. Plunge the comatose lobster into boiling water for about 15 minutes. (Ask your fishmonger for more accurate timings as this depends on the weight of the lobster.) Cool and dress as described.

[MISE-EN-SCENE]

1. Lay the lobster on a chopping board and cut down through the line marked on its head in one downward movement. Straighten the lobster's tail and cut along that too. Remove the claws.

2. Lay the lobster halves next to each other and take out the stomach sac, just behind the mouth, and the dark intestinal tract. Leave the coral and the yellowy green meat as this is lovely to eat.

3. Remove the meat from the claws and place on the lobster. If you want to serve the lobster cold that's fine but you can grill the lobster for 10–15 minutes too. Add a splash of white wine to the lobster to stop it drying out if you are going to do this.

4. To make the sauce, put the lemon juice in a pan. Heat and reduce by half. Whisk in the butter one knob at a time until all the butter is amalgamated. Stir in the parsley and season to taste.

5. Pour over the lobster, put on a bib, eat and enjoy. Save some energy for later, hopefully.

Boeuf Bourguignon

JULIE AND JULIA (2009)

'You can never have too much butter'

[CAST & CREW]

250g (9oz) smoked bacon,
  cut into 1cm (½in)
  strips
1kg (2¼lb) braising
  steak
1 tbsp flour
1 tbsp vegetable oil
1 carrot, cut into batons
1 onion, finely sliced
2 garlic cloves, grated
300ml (½ pint) beef
  stock or consommé
1 tbsp tomato purée
300ml (½ pint) red wine
350g (12oz) button
  mushrooms
6 shallots, peeled and
  halved
1 bay leaf, crumbled
1 sprig fresh thyme
salt and ground black
  pepper
mashed potato and wine,
  to serve

Serves 4

Julia Child's mellifluous voice and refreshing honesty made the culinary impossible seem possible. 'Boning a duck? For goodness sake, pick up the knife and get on with it!' That was her motto, and I wholeheartedly agree.

In the movie, Julia's journey through time to create her 'magnum opus' was a huge undertaking and not without many obstacles. Her sheer joy at receiving a copy of her first published book brought a genuine tear to my eye.

Bon Appétit!

[MISE-EN-SCENE ... WITH APOLOGIES TO JULIA CHILD]

1. Heat the oven to 160°C (140°C fan oven) mark 2½.

2. Heat a frying pan until hot, then add the bacon. Cook, tossing occasionally, until the bacon crisps and the fat is released. Remove the bacon to a large lidded casserole dish, reserving the fat in the frying pan.

3. Pat the steak dry with a paper towel. Cut into 2cm (¾in) cubes. Sprinkle over the flour and toss to coat. Return the frying pan to the heat and fry the beef cubes a few at a time, adding 1 tsp of the oil, if needed. Do not overcrowd the pan or the meat will steam and not brown. Place the browned cubes into the casserole dish and set aside.

4. Add the remaining 2 tsp oil to the pan and gently fry the carrots, onion and garlic until softened, then add to the casserole. Drain any remaining fat from the pan and return to the heat. Pour in the beef stock and warm, scraping any crusty bits from the bottom of the pan using a wooden spoon.

5. Pour the warm stock and tomato purée into the casserole dish, then add enough wine to just cover the contents of the dish. Add the bay leaf and thyme, stir well and heat to a simmer. Cover and bake for 2 hours, stirring every 30 minutes of so. If the casserole becomes dry or the sauce too thick, add a little more wine or water.

6. Add the shallots and mushrooms, season to taste, re-cover and bake for a further 1 hour until the beef is tender and soft enough to be easily broken up with a spoon.

7. Serve with plenty of mashed potato and wine.

[VOICE-OVER]

If you are in a job you can't stand or a country you'd rather leave, get a copy of your favourite cook book and cook your way from cover to cover. Alternatively, write a cook book of your own. It worked for Julia!

'I enjoy a glass of wine while I'm preparing the evening meal...chips and egg'

[CAST & CREW]

500g (1lb 2oz) squid
  tubes, fresh or frozen
  are fine, add tentacles
  too if you like them.
150g (2oz) plain flour
1 tsp smoked paprika
salt and ground black
  pepper
vegetable oil, for
  frying
lemon wedges and fresh
  parsley, chopped, to
  serve

Serves 4 as a starter

Shirley Valentine's life in England is very ordinary except when she spends some evenings talking to the microwave.

However, it's easy to see why the sun, sand and sex in exotic Greece would awaken Shirley to a world of missed opportunities.

With this in mind, Shirley allows moustachioed Costas to take her mind off her boring and unfulfilling English life as he introduces her to the amazing 'F plan diet' where sex is the only ingredient!

Costa's Taverna serves a wide variety of *mezedes*. This is food made perfectly for sharing and only enhances the need to look deeply into the eyes of your vacation squeeze as you ask them to pass you the hummus!

[VOICE-OVER]

Make a complete meal of little dishes. Calamari, olives, good bread and slowly cooked lamb would be a fine place to start. Remember, you don't have to cook all of this yourself. A Greek or Mediterranean deli will always help you to put together a balanced set of mezedes.

[MISE-EN-SCENE]

1. Take each squid tube and wash well. Make sure none of the squid cartilage is still inside the body.

2. You need to decide, rings or rectangles? For rings, slice across the tube at 5mm ($1/4$in) intervals. For rectangles, open up the tube by cutting along one side. Score the squid diagonally in both directions to create a diamond pattern, then slice into 2x3cm (1x1 $1/2$in) rectangles.

3. Heat about 2cm (1in) of oil in a heavy-based pan.

4. Put the flour, paprika, salt and pepper in a plastic bag, then add the squid and give the bag a really good shake to coat.

5. Place a few squid pieces in the pan at a time. Don't add too many as this will cool the oil and the squid rings will be soggy and won't crisp up. As soon as they become golden remove and drain on several layers of kitchen paper. Repeat until all the calamari are cooked.

6. Dust with a little more paprika and serve with lemon wedges, a sprinkle of parsley and a sunset.

7. Choose a few more dishes for your 'F' plan diet.

Chicken Mole

CHOCOLAT (2000)

'Advertise on your own time. What's for dessert?'

[CAST & CREW]

1 chicken, cut into eight portions and skinned
2 dried chillis (smoked if possible)
1 tbsp vegetable oil
1 onion, finely chopped
1 garlic clove
6 very ripe tomatoes, peeled and chopped, or semi-dried sunblush tomatoes
handful of unsalted peanuts
1 tortilla
40g (1^1/$_2$ oz) dark chocolate (minimum 70% cocoa solids)
ground cinnamon
1 fresh green chilli, chopped
fresh coriander

Serves 4

Vianne's role as the new chocolatier in the very insular village of Lansquenet-sous-Tannes acts as a catalyst for personal change in the whole village. This is brought about by Vianne's almost psychic ability to match a person's problem to a particular chocolate cure.

If you've never experienced mole sauce before, I assure you it is a life-changing event. Making this meal for Armande on his birthday, Vianne sets out to ensnare everyone who shares in the feast. The heat from the chilli combining with endorphins from the chocolate will light a passionate fire in you all!

[MISE-EN-SCENE]

1. Place the chicken joints in a pan and cover with water. Bring to a simmer and poach gently for 45 minutes until cooked through. Remove from the pan and cool. Reserve the cooking liquor for later.

2. Meanwhile, in a hot pan dry-fry the dried chillies until they begin to char and blacken. Take them from the pan and place in a small bowl. Using a little of the chicken water cover and leave to soak them for 10-15 minutes. Once re-hydrated remove the seeds.

3. Add a little oil to the pan and gently fry the onions and garlic until they begin to turn a pale golden colour.

4. Place the onions, garlic, tomatoes and dried chillies into a liquidiser and blend. Add the peanuts, dried tortilla and a little more chicken water to loosen, then blitz until smooth. Return to the hot pan.

5. Stir in the chocolate and keep on a low heat until melted. Taste and season. Add the cinnamon to taste, a pinch at a time. Your mole sauce is now ready.

6. Place the poached chicken pieces into a large saucepan, pour over the chocolate mole sauce, add about 300ml ($1/2$ pint) of the reserved chicken stock and put the lid on the pan. Simmer gently for another 25 minutes, stirring occasionally. Check the sauce from time to time, adding a little more of the reserved cooking liquor if needed.

7. Sprinkle over the chopped fresh green chilli and coriander and serve with rice and a wedge of lime to give a little citrus freshness.

[VOICE-OVER]

Very little chocolate is needed to make a difference to this dish. The result should barely taste of chocolate but the depth of flavour will be enhanced greatly. Buy really good-quality chocolate, it makes all the difference.

Lasagna

GARFIELD: THE MOVIE (2004)

'Once again, my life has been saved by the miracle of lasagna'

[CAST & CREW]

1kg (2lb 4oz) beef mince
  or 500g (1lb 2oz) beef
  mince and 500g (1lb
  2oz) veal mince
300ml ($^1/_2$ pint) passata
  (strained tomatoes)
salt and freshly ground
  black pepper
1 onion, chopped
2 sticks of celery,
  chopped
1 carrot, finely chopped
250ml (9fl oz) chicken
  stock
1-2 tbsp olive oil, for
  frying
9-12 lasagna sheets
For the Bechamel sauce:
50g (2oz) flour
50g (2oz) butter
600-900ml (1$^1/_2$ pints)
  milk
salt and white pepper
4-5 tbsp of Parmesan
  cheese

Serves 4-6

For Garfield, the thought of sharing both owner John and, most terrifyingly, his food drives the loveable ginger hero to extreme lengths - locking dim-witted dog Odie out of the house. Of course, Odie is subsequently kidnapped, leading Garfield to shed his normally slothful nature and attempt to return Odie to the bosom of his family.

That doesn't mean Garfield gives up his first love of eating though. During the movie, Garfield manages to devour flavour-blasted goldfish snacks, meatloaf, corned beef hash and, at least, four boxes of very tasting-looking lasagna. Hopefully, this recipe will do the trick for you lot too!

[VOICE-OVER]

Serve with a crisp green salad or, if you happen to be a fat cat, more lasagna. If you really need to belly flop into this dish please allow it to cool a little before doing so. And I'd suggest putting on some elasticated trousers too.

[MISE-EN-SCENE]

1. Shut the kitchen door to thwart any attempts at sabotage by a large ginger tomcat.

2. In a large pan heat the olive oil. Add the onion, celery and carrot, add a sprinkle of salt to prevent the veggies from browning and fry gently until softened. Remove to a dish and keep warm.

3. Place the mince in the pan and keep stirring until browned and cooked through. Add the passata and chicken stock and stir again. Return the vegetables, reduce the temperature and simmer gently for 30 minutes until the liquid has almost reduced completely. Remove from the heat and preheat the oven to 220°C (200°C fan oven) mark 7.

4. Make the Bechamel sauce. Melt the butter over a low heat in a large pan, add the flour and stir for 1 minute. Gradually whisk in the milk and cook, stirring constantly, until the sauce thickens. Once at the thickness you need for your dish cook for about 30 seconds more. Season to taste.

5. Build your lasagna using one third of each ingredient as you go. Add a layer of meat first, then the pasta sheets, and finally a layer of the white sauce. Sprinkle the Parmesan cheese over the top and bake for 20-25 minutes until the edges bubble and the top is browned.

Lemon Lamb

MY BIG FAT GREEK WEDDING (2002)

'There are three things that every Greek woman must do in life: marry Greek boys, make Greek babies, and feed everyone'

[CAST & CREW]

3 lemons, one peeled thinly and juiced, 2 cut into chunks
3 garlic cloves, chopped or crushed
good Greek olive oil (for Toula's father!)
2 tbsp fresh oregano
1 leg of lamb (approx 1.8kg [4lb], butterflied
2 onions, halved and sliced
salt and ground black pepper
greek salad, to serve

Serves 6

Toula's life is complicated. She wants to please her family, marry a good Greek man and raise Greek babies...but it just isn't happening. With her 30th birthday looming, Toula's decision to break out from her family's traditional stranglehold allows her to meet and fall in love with non-Greek Ian. How Toula's food-obsessed, restaurant-owning, mega-family react to her new, vegetarian boyfriend is fantastic. 'It's no problem,' says the bewildered aunt, 'I'll make lamb.'

You can make it too. Simply gather together your family, grab a hunky partner and follow this recipe.

[VOICE-OVER]

If you want to make this for more than 6 people it would make more sense to buy another leg of lamb rather than simply a larger leg. This will keep the cooking time down, ensures the lamb is tender and might, if you are lucky, give you leftovers for the following day.

[MISE-EN-SCENE]

1. Put the lemon peel, juice, garlic, olive oil, oregano, salt and pepper in a bowl. Mix well, then add the lamb. Massage the marinade in with your hands and leave to marinade for at least two hours.

2. Preheat the oven to 240°C (220°C fan oven) mark 9.

3. Scatter the onion and lemon chunks over the base of a large roasting tin. Lay the large leg bone in the bottom of the tin to act as a trivet. Rest the butterflied lamb gently over the top and roast for 25-35 minutes. I know, I know, it seems like a very short time, but trust me - 25 minutes will give you very pink lamb, 35 minutes less so.

4. Remove from the oven and leave to rest for 10 minutes. Meanwhile, strain the juices from the bottom of the roasting tin into a pan. Taste and adjust the seasoning. If you like a thicker gravy stir in a little cornflour mixed with water and keep stirring as you heat to prevent lumps.

5. Carve the lamb into thick slices. Serve with crushed boiled new potatoes, gravy and a big Greek salad on the side.

6. Dance in a big circle as the sun goes down over the pile of empty Ouzo bottles.

250g (9oz) broad beans,
  shelled
a bowl of iced water
splash of vegetable oil
350g (12oz) lambs'
  liver, cleaned, trimmed
  and cut into slices
2 knobs of butter
salt and ground black
  pepper
a glass of nice Chianti,
  to serve

Serves 2

The utterly dead look in Hannibal Lecter's eyes as he recalls the fate of the census-taker is etched in everyone's memory. Indeed, if I ever ask the butcher for liver, I have to stop myself from adding 'with some fava beans and a nice chianti'. I don't do the sinister sucking air through my teeth at the end however.

Though it has sinister connotations, this is a very tasty meal. Especially, as Dr Lecter might say, for anyone who enjoys 'having a friend' for dinner.

[VOICE-OVER]

The season for broad beans is late spring to early summer and that's just the time for new-season lamb too. That could put Clarice off eating this dish - as it is her childhood nightmare that gave way to the title of the film - but don't let that bother you.

[VARIATION]

I'm a purist and however fancy this meal may seem, the best accompaniments to this are a huge pile of creamy mash and caramelised onions. Though I'm sure Lecter would disagree.

[MISE-EN-SCENE]

1. Place the broad beans in unsalted water and bring to the boil for 2-3 minutes. Drain and place in a bowl of iced water. When cold slip the beans out of their skins. If the skins are tough, you may need to nick them with a sharp knife. Pop the bright green beans into a separate bowl.

2. Heat a frying pan until hot and add the oil to the pan. Season the liver with salt and pepper, then briefly cook over a high heat, turning to cook on both sides. Quickly cook the liver over a high heat for a moment or so on each side. The liver should be a little crisp on the outside but still pink in the middle. Add a knob of butter to the pan, turning the liver all the time to coat. Remove from the pan and place on a warm plate to rest.

3. Add the second knob of butter to the pan and when melted toss in the broad beans. Combine well with the butter and liver juices and warm through.

4. Serve the liver and fava beans on a warmed plate with a glass of Chianti. (If you want to you could deglaze the pan with a little Chianti and yet another knob of butter. Reduce down rapidly and serve as a red wine sauce with the liver and beans.)

[CAST & CREW]

oil, for greasing

6 rashers smoked streaky bacon

500g (1lb 2oz) lean beef mince

500g (1lb 2oz) lean pork mince

1 onion, finely chopped

1 stick of celery, finely chopped

1 egg

splash of Worcester sauce or Tabasco

1 tsp Dijon mustard

good squirt of tomato ketchup

big handful of bread crumbs

2 tbsp fresh parsley, chopped

salt and ground black pepper

Serves 4

Meatloaf graces the tables of suburban America from Alaska to Florida. It is the embodiment of average America on a plate. It's also an inexpensive and easy meal to make and is comfort food par excellence – familiar and safe. Much like life in *Pleasantville* before the vivid technicolour of life came and awoke everyone's passion – a collision between the real world and the traditional world of *Pleasantville*. If you've never had meatloaf before, I suggest you give it a try – you will be pleasantly pleased you did.

[SERVING SUGGESTION]

Serve with mash, green beans and a fresh tomato sauce (ketchup if you must) or if it is too colourful then try a meatloaf sandwich.
To make a simple fresh tomato sauce, warm passata with some olive oil and a handful of freshly chopped parsley. Tasty enough to bring the colour to your cheeks – although Jennifer had other methods in the movie, I know. Just ask Skip!

[MISE-EN-SCENE]

1. Preheat the oven to 180°C (160°C fan oven) mark 4. Lightly oil the inside of a 900g (2lb) loaf tin. Lay the bacon rashers on a chopping board and stretch with the back of a heavy knife. Lay the rashers across the tin sideways to line. Don't worry if there is any left hanging over the edge of the tin.

2. In a large bowl combine the mince, onion, celery, egg, Worcestershire sauce or Tabasco, mustard, tomato ketchup, breadcrumbs, parsley and seasoning. Use your hands to really get squidging. (Mary Sue would approve of using your hands in this manner!) The texture of meatloaf should be pretty uniform.

3. Dollop the meatloaf mixture into the bacon-lined tin and press down to ensure there are no air pockets. Cover the top with any of the overhanging bacon and cover with a sheet of foil.

4. Place the loaf tin into a bain marie and bake for 1½ hours. Uncover the meatloaf for the last 20 minutes or so to crisp the bacon on the top of the dish. Once cooked leave to rest for about 10 minutes before slicing.

Meat Pie

SWEENEY TODD (2007)

'Oooh, this tastes lovely, what's your secret ingredient?'

[CAST & CREW]

500g (1lb 2oz) stewing
  steak
2 tbsp vegetable oil
2 tbsp flour
1 tsp mustard powder
1 onion, finely chopped
2 garlic cloves
glass of red wine
beef stock, to cover
2 carrots, chopped
1 tsp horseradish sauce
2 sticks of celery,
  chopped
1/2 pack of 500g pastry,
  rolled to thickness
  of pound coin
1 egg, beaten
salt and ground black
  pepper

Serves 4

In Tim Burton's *Sweeney Todd*, Mrs Lovett and Mr Todd have a far more sinister secret ingredient in their very tasty and addictive pies.

This murderous pair didn't set out to become pioneers in the food world by offering new and exciting flavour combinations to an unsuspecting city of pie-lovers. But they did. Priest in a communion wine gravy or Royal marine and chips were not initially on the menu, but when the opportunity arises, Mrs Lovett spies a tasty way to make money.

The film, with help from Stephen Sondheim's mouth-watering lyrics, is a devilishly dark slice of foodie fun. Enjoy...

[VOICE-OVER]

'It's fop, finest in the shop. Or we have shepherd's pie peppered with actual shepherd on top. And I've just begun. Here's the politician, so oily it's served on a doily, have one'

[SERVING SUGGESTION]

Use up any scraps of pastry to decorate the top of your pie. Leaf shapes and lattices are popular. If you are artistic you could make a decoration that reflects the filling. Maybe a vicar's collar? A judge's gavel? Or even a shepherd's crook? I'll leave the choices of filling up to you.

[MISE-EN-SCENE]

1. Cut the steak into cubes. Place flour and mustard powder into a bowl and season well. Add the meat and toss to coat well. Set aside for a few minutes.

2. Heat the oil in a large pan, add the floured beef and cook until well-browned. Remove and set to one side. Add the onions to the pan with a little more oil if needed, continue to cook out until the onions have softened but not taken on any colour. Tip in the garlic towards the end and soften this too. Add the onions and garlic to the meat, leaving the pan empty.

3. Add the wine to the pan and scrape up the crusty bits, then add the meat and onions back and pour over stock to cover. Bring to a bare simmer, reduce the heat, cover and cook for 2 hours stirring occasionally.

4. After two hours, check the seasoning and add the carrots, horseradish and celery. Cover again and leave for a further 30 minutes.

5. Meanwhile preheat the oven to 200℃ (180℃ fan oven) mark 6.

6. Place the cooked beef mixture into a baking dish and top with the pastry, trimming to fit the dish.

7. Brush the topping with beaten egg and bake for 25-30 minutes until golden brown. Don't tell anyone your secret ingredient.

Pancakes, Bacon and Maple Syrup

GROUNDHOG DAY (1993)

'Don't mess with me, porkchop'

[CAST & CREW]

8 rashers streaky bacon
125g (4oz) plain flour
1 tsp baking powder
pinch of salt
2 eggs
200ml (7fl oz)
  buttermilk
  (alternatively combine
  200ml (7fl oz) milk
  with 3 tsp lemon juice
  and leave to stand for
  10 minutes)
vegetable oil spray
maple syrup, warmed, to
  serve

Makes 8 pancakes

Safe in the knowledge there will be no tomorrow, Phil Connors indulges in his deepest, darkest breakfast fantasies and eats it all in one calorific sitting.

Groundhog Day's constant and relentless narrative monotony mounts up until one day Phil asks the nice-but-dim owner of the hotel he is staying at, 'Do you ever have déjà vu, Mrs Lancaster?'

'I don't think so,' comes the reply, 'but I could check with the kitchen.'

[VOICE-OVER]

If the idea of syrup on bacon is a step too far, then you can buy some very good maple-cured bacon. This will give you that slightly sweet flavour as a foil for the saltier pancakes without the sickly stickiness that can be a little cloying.

[CALORIE-O-METER]

This fantastically indulgent meal racks up about 750 calories of a person's recommended 2000 per day – and that's if you go easy on the butter and syrup!

[MISE-EN-SCENE]

1. Preheat oven to 190℃ (170℃ fan oven) mark 5. Lay the strips of bacon on a wire rack and place in a roasting tin. Bake for 15-20 minutes until cooked to your liking.

2. Meanwhile, sieve the flour and baking powder into a large bowl, add the salt and stir to combine.

3. Whisk in the eggs one at a time, then whisk in the milk a little at a time until the batter is the consistency of yogurt. Leave to stand for 10-15 minutes.

4. Heat a heavy-based frying pan and spray with a little oil. When the oil appears to be rippling, drop tablespoons of the batter on to the pan. Cook until little bubbles rise to the surface, then turn and cook on the other side. Remove to a plate and keep warm until all the pancakes are cooked.

5. Serve several large pancakes with crispy bacon and lashings of maple syrup. Unless you are stuck in the *Groundhog Day* loop I'd suggest this breakfast is a rare treat not a daily ritual.

Pease Pudding & Saveloy

OLIVER! (1968)

'Please Sir, I want some more'

[CAST & CREW]

125g (4oz) yellow split
  peas
water or ham stock, to
  cover
1 onion
2 or 3 sprigs of thyme
1 garlic clove
2 saveloys
knob of butter
square of muslin and
  butcher's string

Serves 2

The workhouse boys in *Oliver!* waiting for their daily bowl of gruel, have barely enough food to sustain them. However, they let their imaginations run riot by dreaming of sausages, jelly and steak.

These malnourished boys pick at straws to decide who will ask Fagin for more. Oliver's fate is sealed by the shortest of straws.

To be perfectly honest, pease pudding and saveloy wouldn't have been much more expensive than gruel but as a meal it is significantly more filling than the tasteless slop they were served.

[VOICE-OVER]

If you can't find muslin then an old, scrupulously clean handkerchief or a new but washed J-cloth will be a perfectly adequate substitute. Tie the bundle to the pan handle with the butcher's string to stop the pudding bobbing about and splitting into the stock.

[MISE-EN-SCENE]

1. Soak the peas overnight in cold water. Take out any that don't swell or that look odd. You will know!

2. Drain and rinse the peas, then place them in a pan and cover well with water or ham stock. Remove the skin from the onion and garlic, then add to the pan with the thyme and bring to a rapid boil. Boil for 10 minutes, then skim the pot and reduce to a gentle simmer for 1 hour 20 minutes.

3. Strain the split peas into a bowl, reserving the cooking liquor. Remove the onion, thyme and garlic and discard. Rub the peas through a sieve and place the purée in the centre of the large muslin square. Tie the top with butcher's string to make a round pudding.

4. Return the stock to the pan, add the saveloy and lower in the muslin-wrapped peas. Simmer for a further hour.

5. Remove the pease pudding from the muslin and beat in a knob of butter. If very stiff add a little ham stock to loosen the mixture. Serve with the saveloy.

6. Hopefully, this will not give you indigestion.

7. Beware of small boys pleading to lick the bowl.

You're nothing but a smear on the sports page to me,
you slimy, ugly, intestinal parasite! Eat me! Eat me!'

[CAST & CREW]

300g (11oz) plain flour
pinch of salt
1 egg
4 tsp sour cream
6 tbsp warm water
soured cream and melted
  butter, to serve

For the filling
50g (2oz) butter, melted
$1/2$ onion, finely chopped
300g (11oz) cold mashed
  potato
150g (5oz) cottage
  cheese
salt and ground black
  pepper

Makes about 40 dumplings

Pity poor old Mr Rosenberg, the jeweller with the
cat, and his humongous Arquillian associate –
assassinated by the film's bug villain before they
even had a chance to eat their food. Now, as a
committed foodie like me, falling face forward into
a large bowl of Pierogi, as this pair of aliens did,
is not a bad way to die ... but I'd want to have eaten
the contents first!

[MISE-EN-SCENE]

1. Have your house checked and fumigated to ensure no bugs crawl out of the woodwork to spoil your fun.

2. Sift the flour and salt into a large bowl. Make a little well in the centre and add the egg and sour cream. Using a fork gradually work the egg and sour cream into the flour.

3. Stir in the warm water a little at a time until well mixed and just a little tacky to the touch. (Don't worry if you don't use all the water.) Set aside to rest for about 30 minutes with a clean cloth in a warm place.

4. Meanwhile, make the filling. Melt the butter in a pan, then add the onion and fry gently for about 5 minutes until softened and translucent, but not coloured. Leave to cool for about 5 minutes.

5. In a separate bowl combine the mashed potato and cottage cheese. Stir in the cooled onion and melted butter and season to taste.

6. Bring a large pan of salted water to the boil. Meanwhile, roll the dough to about 3mm thick and cut into 7cm rounds, using a tumbler or cookie cutter. Lay a round of dough in the palm of your hand and place a teaspoonful of filling on to one half of the dough. Fold the other side over to make a half circle. Pinch the edges together firmly.

7. Gently drop the pierogi into the water and cover (ideally with a glass lid). Simmer for 3-4 minutes until the dumplings rise to the surface. Drain and serve immediately with a little melted butter and a dollop of soured cream. (Leftover pierogi can be left to cool for reheating later.)

[VOICE-OVER]

Pierogi are even better reheated. Melt a little butter in a pan and fry for a moment or two on each side until the filling is heated through and the dumpling becomes crisp and golden. Crispy bacon, fried mushrooms and slow-cooked fried onions are delicious scattered over the final dish.

Pizza

MYSTIC PIZZA (1988)

'What the hell do you think Leona puts in that pizza?'

[CAST & CREW]

2 tbsp olive oil
1 garlic clove, crushed
500g (1lb 2oz) carton of
  strained tomatoes
1 tsp piri piri sauce
about 1 tsp sugar
1 tbsp fresh chopped
  parsley
1 bay leaf
1 ball of fresh
  mozzarella, sliced
a handful of fresh basil
  leaves
salt and ground black
  pepper
For the dough
300ml (¹/₂ pint) warm
  water
1 tbsp caster sugar
10g (or 4 heaped tsps)
  dried active yeast
500g (1lb 2oz) strong
  white bread flour,
large pinch of salt
1¹/₂ tbsp olive oil

Serves 4

The summer JoJo, Daisy and Cat spend working Mystic Pizza together is full of love, loss, lust...and, of course, pizza.

Leona, the restaurant's owner, has a secret tomato sauce recipe that has travelled all the way from the Algarve and she guards it with her life. It would have been nice to find out how she made it; you wish the filmmakers could have given the recipe in the credits at the end!

With or without the threat of the goat's cheese topping (go watch the movie!) this pizza recipe is, in the words of the Fireside Gourmet, 'Superb'.

A slice of heaven, indeed...

[MISE-EN-SCENE]

1. First make the dough. Pour 150ml (50fl oz) of the warm water into a large jug. Add the sugar and yeast and give a brisk stir. Leave in a warm, draught-free place until the mixture becomes frothy.

2. Sift the flour into a large bowl, then add the salt and oil. Pour the frothy yeast mixture and two-thirds of the remaining water into the flour. Shape one hand into a claw and gradually combine the flour and the liquids. Slowly add the remaining tepid water until the dough is soft to the touch, and neither dry nor sticky.

3. Dust the work surface with flour and knead the dough for 5-10 minutes until smooth and soft. Return the dough to the bowl, cover with a clean tea towel and leave in a warm place for about 1 hour until doubled in size.

4. Meanwhile, make the sauce. Heat the olive oil in a pan, then gently fry the garlic for about 1 minute, being careful not to let it burn. Add the passata and stir in the piri piri sauce. Season with the salt, pepper and sugar to taste. (The sugar will heighten the tomato flavour not sweeten the dish.)

5. Leave the sauce to simmer gently until reduced by half, then remove from the heat and stir in the parsley. Add the bay leaf and press down into the sauce. Leave to cool.

6. When the dough has risen, thump it in the middle to knock it back. Divide the dough into four balls, cover with a clean tea towel and leave to rise again for 30 minutes.

7. Meanwhile, preheat the oven to 240°C (220°C fan oven) mark 9. Remove the bay leaf from the sauce and discard, then give the sauce a quick stir. Roll each ball of dough into a 20cm (8in) round and arrange on baking sheets. Spread each one with a thin layer of sauce. Scatter over the mozzarella and basil leaves, and sprinkle over a good grinding of black pepper.

8. Bake for about 10 minutes until golden and bubbling. Drizzle with olive oil, cut into wedges and eat with your hands.

1 rabbit, cut into eight
  portions
2 tbsp flour
2 tbsp vegetable oil
4 rashers streaky bacon,
  chopped
1 onion, finely chopped
2 sticks celery, chopped
1 garlic clove, crushed
1 glass red wine
water or chicken stock,
  to cover
1 carrot, finely chopped
bunch of fresh thyme
salt and ground black
  pepper

Serves 4

Something should have twigged inside Michael Douglas'
head when the very devious Glenn Close invited him
over for dinner with the words, 'Bring the dog, I
love animals...I'm a great cook.' Little did he know.

One of the many great things about this
psychological thriller is that it created the phrase
'bunny boiler', now synonymous with crazy, stalker
exes the world over. Despite this, the movie has been
credited with saving many marriages. One reason might
be explained by Tom Hanks' reference to it in
Sleepless in Seattle where he exclaims, 'Well I saw
it! It scared the shit outta me! It scared the shit
outta every man in America!'

[VOICE-OVER]

Cooking rabbit needs a watchful eye. It is hard to say exactly how long the stew will take to cook because it depends on how much exercise the bunny has done. Wild rabbits take longer, pampered bunnies purloined from hutches will take less time to cook – although this is not a recommendation on my part.

[MISE-EN-SCENE]

1. Source your rabbit with care but don't just raid a former lover's rabbit hutch in revenge.

2. Place flour into a bowl and season well. Toss the rabbit in the flour to coat. Set aside for a few minutes.

3. Heat the oil in a large pan, add the rabbit and cook until the rabbit pieces are golden. Remove to a plate and leave to rest.

4. Add the bacon to the pan and cook until crispy, then add the onions, celery and garlic and cook until the onions are golden and melting. Tip in any remaining seasoned flour and cook for one minute, then add the rabbit. Pour in the wine and allow the alcohol to cook off for a moment or two.

5. Add water or stock to cover and bring to simmering point. Add the carrot and thyme. Reduce the heat, cover and cook for about 1½ hours, stirring occasionally.

6. Take a piece of rabbit and test that it has cooked through to the bone, check the seasoning. Remove any visible small bones to serve. The mashed potatoes soak up the deep red gravy and will look gory-making the dish an appropriate homage to a truly scary film.

Roast Quail

BABETTE'S FEAST (1987)

*'Amazing... an amontillado! And the finest amontillado
I have ever tasted!'*

[CAST & CREW]

500g (17oz) packet
  ready-made puff pastry
1 egg, beaten
4 quail
knob of butter, plus
  extra
1 tbsp vegetable oil,
  plus extra
200g (7oz) fois gras
  (optional, the meal in
  the film has fois gras
  and you can have too if
  you can afford it)
16 strips pancetta
  torn into pieces
1 shallot, chopped
250g (9oz) wild
  mushrooms, sliced
salt and ground black
  pepper

Serves 4

Roast Quail? I know what you're thinking - too much effort? You may be right. But for Babette, in this fabulous food-for-thought movie, Babette's desire to thank the two sisters who helped her out by cooking a delicious meal, ends up raising their spiritual outlook and broadening their horizons through new tastes and experiences.

Much has been said about the spirituality and metaphor in this film, however, if you can cook this feast and give your friends as much pleasure as Babette gives her guests, then that's all that matters.

[MISE-EN-SCENE]

1. Heat the oven to 200°C (180°C fan oven) mark 6. Roll out the pastry to about 3mm (1/8in) thick. Cut out four 10cm (4in) rounds. Score a line about 1.5cm 1/3in) from the edge of each round, being careful not to cut right through the pastry.

2. Brush the edges of the pastry circles with beaten egg and bake in the oven for 10-15 minutes, or until golden brown. Allow to cool. Remove the inside round of each pastry to make a large vol-au-vent. Increase the oven temperature to 220°C (200°C fan oven) mark 7.

3. If the quails still have their heads, remove (although you can always ask your butcher to do this for you). Using a sharp kitchen knife cut down one side of the bird's backbone. Do the same to the other side and remove the backbone completely. Repeat with remaining birds, then wash and pat dry and season inside.

4. Heat the knob of butter and 1 tbsp oil in a pan, then add the quail and brown until golden. Reserve the butter in the pan.

5. Press the quail back into shape. Place 50g (2oz) fois gras into each bird if using. Arrange in a roasting tin and lay the pancetta slices onto the breast and legs of the birds. Roast for 10 minutes, then set aside to rest for 5 minutes.

6. Meanwhile, sauté the shallot in the reserved butter until they just begin to colour, adding a little more butter or oil if needed. Add the mushrooms and cook until they start to give out their liquid. Carry on cooking until the liquid has evaporated.

7. Place a pastry shell on each plate. Layer a quarter of the mushrooms into each shell. Top with the quail and spoon over any juices in the roasting tin or on the resting plate.

[VOICE-OVER]

You can buy excellent packs of puff pastry from the supermarket, although buy the one made with all-butter. Whether you buy the ready-rolled or the block to roll yourself it doesn't matter. Personally, if you are going to the effort of boning a quail you can bloody well summon up the enthusiasm to roll out some pastry!

Scallops with Saffron Sauce

NO RESERVATIONS (2007)

'I wish there was a cookbook for life, you know?
Recipes telling us exactly what to do'

[CAST & CREW]

12 scallops, cleaned

For the sauce:
4 shallots, finely chopped
4 kaffir lime leaves, finely sliced
1 lemon, zested and juiced (you need about 75ml (2 ½ fl oz) lemon juice)
75ml (2 ½ fl oz) good white wine
pinch of saffron threads
100ml double cream
125g (4oz) unsalted butter (salted will do, but be careful when seasoning), diced
2 tsp fresh parsley, chopped
salt and ground black pepper

I really wanted to dislike this Hollywood remake of the German movie *Bella Martha* but the hardcore gastro porn won me over with all that talk of gently roasted quails, bowls of simple tomato pasta and thick juicy steaks cooked to perfection.

My favourite scene is when Kate is fed sauce from a tiny copper saucepan by Nick. Not because I fancy Nick but because I want a set of those tiny copper pans!

[VOICE-OVER]

Fresh scallops are always best but if that just isn't possible, then frozen are always a good alternative. This sauce will work with other white fish that has been simply pan-fried or grilled. If anyone criticises, remember that the customer is always right!

[MISE-EN-SCENE]

1. Place the shallots, kaffir lime leaves, lemon juice and white wine in a pan and bring slowly to the boil. Bubble to reduce until you have about 2 tbsp of mush in the bottom of the pan. Leave to cool slightly.

2. Add the saffron threads to the cream and set aside to infuse.

3. Place the shallot mixture over a very low flame and whisk in the butter a few knobs at a time. You need to keep whisking as this traps the air bubbles in the butter and makes the sauce light and emulsified.

4. Drizzle a little oil into a frying pan and heat until very hot. Season the scallops and place in the pan. Cook for only a minute or so on each side until the scallops lose their translucency.

5. Whilst the scallops cook finish the sauce. Stir in the saffron cream, chopped parsley and check the seasoning.

6. Serve the scallops with the sauce, a scattering of parsley and lemon zest and a lemon or lime wedge on the side. Do not question the chef's cooking.

Seafood Risotto

BIG NIGHT (1996)

'Sometimes the spaghetti likes to be alone'

[CAST & CREW]

1 litre (1 ³/₄ pints)
 vegetable stock
500g (1lb 2oz) raw
 prawns, shelled and
 de-veined (reserve the
 shells)
several knobs of butter
splash of olive oil
¹/₂ onion or 2 shallots,
 finely chopped
350g (12oz) risotto rice
150ml (¹/₄ pint) white
 wine
12 small scallops
freshly grated Parmesan
 cheese, to serve
 (optional)

salt and ground black
 pepper

Serves 4

Primo's masterly ways with food are not always understood by his customers – all they want is a sanitised version of Italian food. Despite these frustrations, Primo concocts some truly magnificent dishes. In fact, the entire movie is a visual buffet for the eyes and stomach!

Surprisingly, out of all Primo's dishes on display, it is the simple risotto that caught my eye. Risottos so often make a restaurant's menu complete, even if they are sometimes overlooked.

As Primo so succinctly puts it: 'To eat good food is to be close to God.'

[MISE-EN-SCENE]

1. Pour the stock into a pan and heat to just below simmering point. Add the prawn shells and simmer gently for 15 minutes. Strain the stock into a clean pan and keep warm. Discard the prawn shells and keep warm.

2. Put a knob of butter and a splash of olive oil in a large pan, then add the onion or shallots and fry gently for about 5 minutes until soft but not browned. Stir in the rice and turn to coat in the oil, butter and onion mixture. Stir for about 1 minute until the rice becomes translucent and shiny.

3. Add the white wine and a ladleful of stock. Simmer, stirring constantly, until the liquid has been absorbed. Add another ladleful of stock and continue cooking and stirring in this way until you have almost run out of stock. Taste the rice; it should have a slight al dente bite.

4. In a separate large pan, heat a little more oil and butter and fry the prawns for 3-5 minutes, or until pink. Keep an eye on the risotto as the prawns cook.

5. Add the last slosh of stock to the risotto, season and cook out for a moment or two. Stir in a final knob of butter and season to taste. Stir the cooked prawns into the risotto. (If you like, stir in a good grating of Parmesan but note that Italians very rarely add cheese to seafood dishes.)

6. Wipe out the prawn pan with a piece of kitchen paper and return to the heat. Add a little oil and a knob more butter and heat for a minute or two. Cook the scallops for 30 seconds or so on each side until a light golden colour.

7. Spoon the risotto into four deep bowls and top each portion with three scallops.

[VOICE-OVER]

It is essential that the stock is hot and close at hand when you make risotto. The risotto needs to be stirred well too and this can be tiring. Family members are often a source of free labour for this task, a glass of something cold and Italian may ease the pain.

'I'm on this new diet. Well, I don't eat anything and when I feel like I'm about to faint I eat a cube of cheese. I'm just one stomach flu away from my goal weight'

[CAST & CREW]

400g (14oz) T-bone steak
groundnut oil, for
  frying
1 garlic clove,
  flattened
rosemary sprig
  (optional)
salt and ground black
  pepper
wilted spinach, to serve

Serves 1

Living in the *haute couture* world of Miranda Priestly (Meryl Streep) must be hungry work. Though no one ever seems to eat!

In a heart-breeaking scene from this guilty pleasure movie, Andi, one of Miranda's flunkies at *Runway* magazine, is ordered out to Smith and Wollensky's to bag a thick, sizzling T-bone and speed it back to the office. On screen, the steak looks to-die-for – you just want to reach out and grab it. And I know I wasn't the only one in the cinema to feel real sadness when this beautiful steak was thrown into the sink untouched as Miranda storms out of the office.

This sizzling steak recipe may go unloved by Miranda ... but for the rest of us who enjoy a calorie or ten, then nothing, *nothing*, beats a well-cooked, juicy steak.

[VOICE-OVER]

To wilt spinach, wash the baby spinach leaves and pick out any that have slightly woody stems. Shake off as much water as possible and drop into a dry pan with a knob of butter. The water on the leaves and the little amount of butter should be enough to steam the spinach until it wilts. Serve with a little grate of nutmeg. Baby red or rainbow chard leaves makes a pretty alternative to spinach.

[MISE-EN-SCENE]

1. Buy the best steak you can afford. (You, unlike Miranda, will be eating this so splash out.) Look for the marbling through the steak as this gives it flavour and added succulence.

2. Heat a heavy-based frying pan until very hot but not quite smoking.

3. Put a slug or two of oil in the pan, just enough to coat the pan base. Toss in the flattened garlic clove and rosemary if using and fry for 1 minute. Remove the garlic and rosemary before they burn.

4. Season the steak and lay in the pan. Cook for 1½-3 minutes on the first side, without moving the steak. Turn and repeat this on the second side. (These timings will give you a very rare steak at 1½ minutes to virtually cremated at 3 minutes.

5. Remove the steak to a warm plate and leave to rest for 1-2 minutes. This is vital as it allows the meat to relax. In the same way that your backside would tense up if dropped into a hot pan, steaks do the same!

6. If serving to the fashion conscious, a side of wilted spinach and a glass of San Pellegrino will suffice. If it's for me wilt the spinach in butter and serve with a dish of chunky chips twice-cooked in duck fat. Throw in a decent glass of red and an elasticated waistband and you've got yourself a great evening meal.

Mama Joe's Cornbread

SOUL FOOD (1997)

'Bless this bread, bless this meat, bless this belly 'cause I's gon' eat!'

[CAST & CREW]

75g (3oz) plain flour
75g (3oz) cornmeal
1 heaped tsp baking
  powder
pinch of salt
50g (2oz) butter, plus
  extra for greasing
1 egg, beaten
125ml (4fl oz) full fat
  milk
2 tbsp honey

Serves 4

Family meals are places where home truths are told, lessons are learned and the plot of the story thickens more than any gravy on the table.

Ahmad realises that the family's weekly sessions of bickering and sibling rivalry are actually the glue that holds the family together. Mama Joe believes that fried chicken and cornbread will cure any ill but unfortunately, this isn't always so. When a tragedy befalls Mama Joe, the family begins to fall apart. Ahmad knows that there is only one way to repair his broken-hearted and collapsing family – Mama Joe's soul food!

[VOICE-OVER]

Cornbread is the ideal solution to sopping up the meat juices or any chicken gravy left over. However, it is also a fantastic (but very filling) snack on its own.

[MISE-EN-SCENE]

1. Sift the dry ingredients into a large bowl.

2. Melt the butter over a low heat, then add to the dry mixture with the egg, milk and honey.

3. Combine quickly. Don't worry if there are a few lumps, but be careful not to overwork the mixture.

4. Preheat the oven to 200°c (180°c fan oven) mark 6. Place the dough in a 15x15cm (6x6in) greased baking tray and bake for 20-25 minutes until risen and golden.

5. Wait for a moment or so but consume with enthusiasm.

Spaghetti Sauce
with Wafer Thin Garlic and Meatballs

GOODFELLAS (1990)

*'I ordered some spaghetti with marinara sauce,
and I got egg noodles and ketchup.*

[CAST & CREW]

250g (9oz) minced beef
250g (9oz) minced pork
250g (9oz) minced veal
100g (3^1/$_2$ oz) fresh
  breadcrumbs
1 egg, beaten
1 tbsp olive oil, plus
  extra
1 onion, finely chopped
  (by all means use the
  three suggested by
  Vinnie, but I find it
  too many)
2 garlic cloves, very
  finely sliced
2 400g (14oz) cans
  peeled, chopped
  tomatoes
salt and ground black
  pepper
8 fresh basil leaves, to
  garnish
Parmesan, grated or
  shaved, to serve

I was totally mesmerised the first time I saw Paulie
Cicero slice garlic so uniquely in *Goodfellas*.
Paulie seems to get the slices finer using his razor
blade than I do using a mandolin slicer!

Life for these wise guys in prison, despite the
obvious lack of freedom, appears very comfortable —
lobster, wine and other home comforts are on offer to
to keep them from losing it.

Martin Scorsese's mother's Goodfellas sauce — as
used in the movie — is a family favourite now and as
a result I may need to invest in a blade myself.

This recipe serves four.

[VOICE-OVER]

Never feel any guilt over using tinned tomatoes. Very rarely in the UK will the fresh tomatoes have the same depth of flavour or pulpiness that a rich sugo like this requires. Unless you live in Southern Europe and have access to unrefrigerated, in-season Roma or San Marzano tomatoes, a tin of tomatoes from your local supermarket is your best, and a thoroughly acceptable, option.

[MISE-EN-SCENE]

1. In a large bowl combine all the mince, breadcrumbs, egg and seasoning until well mixed.

2. Using damp hands pinch off walnut-size pieces of mixture and roll into balls.

3. Heat the oil in a large frying pan and add the meatballs. Cook, without stirring for 5 minutes, then turn gently every few minutes until all the sides are browned. Remove to a plate and leave to one side.

4. Using the meat juices in the pan, add the onions and garlic. You may need to add more olive oil at this point. Cook slowly. (Paulie expected the garlic to liquefy in the pan and a slow gentle heat will help this disintegration. You wouldn't want to disappoint him when he has that blade so close by!)

5. Add the tomatoes, bring to a simmer, then reduce the heat. Keep the heat low and stir occasionally until the tomato has softened and the sauce becomes smooth and lump-free.

6. Pop the meatballs back into the tomato sauce and heat through for 5 minutes. Serve with long spaghetti and scatter with freshly torn basil and freshly grated or shaved Parmesan.

7. Play 'Beyond the Sea' (Sinatra's version, of course) whilst enjoying your luxurious penitentiary dinner.

Roast Venison

THE DEER HUNTER (1978)

'A deer has to be taken with one shot. I try to tell people that but they don't listen'

[CAST & CREW]

1 rolled haunch of
venison (1.5 kg)
For the marinade:
1 bottle of red wine
2 tsp peppercorns
1 tsp juniper berries
1 clove of garlic
crushed
sprig of rosemary
sprig of thyme
Roasting ingredients:
8 rashers smoked streaky
bacon
1 onion roughly chopped
2 carrots peeled and
chopped
2 sticks of celery
chopped
salt and pepper
3 tsp rowan or
redcurrant jelly
1 tbsp flour

Serves 4-6

Men who dip Twinkies in mustard and wash them down
with can after can of lukewarm beer are possibly not
connoisseurs of the finer things in life, however
with the unknown terror of Vietnam looming in front
of them they can be easily forgiven.

The boys' last deer hunt in the peace and
tranquillity of the hills, where one shot is all it
takes, is juxtaposed with the brutality and constant
senseless gunfire of the war in Vietnam.

The boys' trophy from the hunt seems only to be the
antlers of the deer as, for them, the thrill of the
chase, rather than that of the kill, was what it was
all about. If you don't fancy Twinkies and mustard
then try this roast venison instead.

[MISE-EN-SCENE]

1. The day before you want to cook the venison pour in three-quarters of the bottle of wine into a large non metallic bowl. Keep the last quarter of a bottle to make the gravy.

2. Place the remaining marinade ingredients into a pestle and mortar and bruise to release their essential oil. If you don't have a pestle and mortar then pop the ingredients into a plastic bag and give them a whack with a rolling pin. Add the bashed about herbage to the wine.

3. Lay the venison into the marinade, cover and place in the fridge overnight.

4. Heat the oven to 190° (170℃ fan oven)/ Gas 5.

5. Roughly chop the onion, carrots and celery and lay in the bottom of a roasting tin. Season well with salt and pepper.

6. Remove the venison from the marinade and pat dry with kitchen towels. Lay the venison onto the vegetable trivet.

7. Place the streaky bacon over the venison haunch strip by strip, covering as much of the surface as possible. This bacon will baste the meat as it cooks.

8. Place in the oven and roast for 20 to 25 minutes per 500g.

9. Once cooked, remove from the roasting dish and allow to rest for 15 minutes. Use this time to make a gravy. Venison isn't that fatty but the bacon was, so tip out almost all the fat from the pan, leave only 1 tbsp of fat in the bottom. Don't remove the vegetables yet as they will add flavour to the gravy.

10. Put the roasting tray over a gentle heat. Stir the flour and cook out for a minute. Once cooked out gradually stir in the remaining unused wine. Scrape any tasty bits from the bottom of the pan as you do so. Add this wine a little at a time until the gravy is the thickness you like.

11. Add the rowan or redcurrant jelly and allow to melt into the gravy. Strain out vegetables from the gravy through a sieve and into a warmed gravy boat.

Thanksgiving Dinner

PLANES, TRAINS AND AUTOMOBILES (1987)

'It feels like a whopper. Turn me over, I'm done on this side. I'm afraid to look at my ass. There'll be griddle marks'

[CAST & CREW]

3kg (6lb) turkey
4 medium sweet potatoes,
  peeled and quartered
8 medium potatoes,
  peeled and diced
500g (1lb 2oz) carrots,
  peeled and cut into
  batons
250g (9oz) green beans
generous amount of
  butter
1 lemon, halved
  (optional)
8 bacon rashers
cream, to taste
1-2 tsp sugar
500g (1lb 2oz) stuffing
cranberry sauce
bread rolls to serve

Serves 4

It only takes one thing to completely ruin your journey plans. Sadly for Steve Martin's character Neal, he is subject to a whole raft of separate disasters seemingly conspiring to prevent him from getting home for Thanksgiving with his family.

Add Del – Neal's incompetent travelling companion – into the mix and you've got yourself a classic comedy scenario.

Indulge yourself and your family with this traditional celebration meal. As Neal would agree, it really is worth the effort.

[MISE-EN-SCENE]

1. Read the label on the turkey as almost all supermarkets put oven temperatures and timings on their packaging these days. If you have bought your bird from a butcher ask their advice on cooking. I use 20 minutes per 450g (1lb) plus an extra 20 minutes.

2. Write down the cooking time of the turkey and add 20 minutes resting time. Work out when you want to eat and when the turkey must go into the oven. Next work out a schedule for the accompaniments: allow 50 minutes to 1 hour to bake sweet potatoes or longer for casseroled potatoes or a gratin and 30 minutes for mashed potatoes.

3. If you want to prepare the root vegetables in advance, put in a large bowl and cover with cold water to prevent discolouration.

4. Fifteen minutes before you are ready to start cooking, preheat the oven to 180℃ (160℃ fan oven) mark 5.

5. Season the turkey with salt and pepper. You can also massage it with butter and shove a lemon into its nether regions if you like. (Stuffing is always better cooked on a separate dish.)

6. At the correct time, bake the sweet potatoes for 50 minutes to 1 hour until tender. Alternatively, make your family recipe for sweet potato casserole or gratin.

7. Consult your list to check that you haven't forgotten anything, put a rasher or several of bacon over the turkey breast and legs to prevent them from over-cooking.

8. Boil the potatoes until tender, then drain well. Mash using a potato ricer to give a smooth finish and beat in loads of butter and cream.

9. When the turkey is cooked and resting, cook the vegetables and gravy. Put the carrots in a pan with 2 tbsp water. Add the sugar and a large knob of butter. Cover, bring to a simmer and cook until tender. The liquid should have evaporated and will leave the carrots with a sticky glaze. Steam the green beans for about 4 minutes until tender.

10. Serve and wash down with wine and your loving family.

Poutine

DINER (1982)

'Suddenly, life was more than french fries, gravy and girls'

[CAST & CREW]

Roasting dish containing
  cooking residues
1 tbsp plain flour,
500ml (17fl oz) warm
  stock choose one that
  matches the roast you
  are cooking,
125ml (4fl oz) wine –
  whatever you are
  drinking with your meal

Serves 4

Avoiding the realities of life by hanging about with
like-minded truth dodgers is all part of growing up.
For five boys living in Baltimore in the late 1950's
the place where they manage to hide longest is the
Diner. Warm and well-fed they discuss the important
issues of the day, mostly their sex lives, either
real or concocted. Venturing out to the cinema, on a
date or occasionally back home, they all seem
happiest when wrapped in the warm fug of the diner.
  You can recreate the same warmth and safety with
this order of chips with gravy, sometimes exotically
called poutine.

[VOICE-OVER]

The golden rule of thumb I stick to when I make poutine is too make sure the gravy is thick enough to stick to the chips when you lift them off the plate. There's nothing worse than watery gravy, that makes the crunchy chips go all soggy.

[SERVING SUGGESTION]

For the perfect French fry recipe to accompany this gravy, flip on over to Happy Days on p168.

[MISE-EN-SCENE]

1. When you roast your joint of meat put some vegetables and woody herbs under it to act both as a trivet to keep the meat out of the fat and also to provide additional flavour for your gravy.

2. Tip the pan and drain the fat and juices to one corner of the pan. Remove the majority of the fat. I aim to leave about 1-2 tablespoons of fat in the pan.

3. Place the roasting tin on a very low heat on the hob and tip in the flour. Using a wooden spoon or a whisk cook the fat and flour together to create a paste. As you do, scrape all the tasty dark bits up from the bottom of the pan.

4. After a minute of cooking take out the floury taste and add a glass of wine (whatever you are drinking with the meal) to the tray and allow to bubble, now add the warm stock a little at a time until all incorporated. You may not need it all, stop when the gravy is the thickness your family likes. If the gravy looks too thin don't panic there is a solution.

5. Pass the gravy through a sieve to remove the vegetable bits and any lumps. If it looks too thin return to a pan and reduce down until the gravy has thickened. Taste and season with salt and pepper.

6. Stir in any additional flavours such as mustard for beef or redcurrant jelly for lamb.

7. Pour over anything and everything.

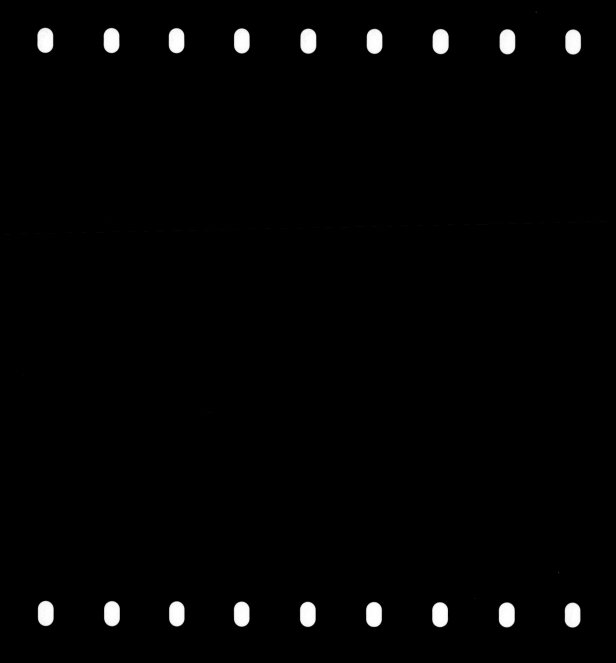

Sequels

Room for seconds?
We've got these fabulous following
acts for you to polish off...

Apple Pie

AMERICAN PIE (1999)

'McDonald's or homemade?'

[CAST & CREW]

250g (9oz) plain flour
125g (4oz) butter or
 margarine
4-6 tbsp cold water
3-4 large Bramley apples
1 tsp cinnamon
sugar, to taste
single cream, to serve

Makes 4

For four teenage boys from Michigan, the result of
peer pressure was to create one of the funniest movie
scenes of all time. Squirming with embarrassment as
we recall our own adolescent fumbling, we watch Jim
attempt third base with an apple pie. My recipe is
for four individual apple pies, one each for Jim,
Finch, Oz and the Stifmeister.

And in answer to Jim's hopeless question, the pies
are homemade, not McDonalds.

[VOICE-OVER]

Despite what this film might lead you to believe, the hole in the pastry topping of any pie is to let the steam escape. This allows the pie crust to crisp up and become golden in the oven.

[MISE-EN-SCENE]

1. Preheat oven to 200°C (180°C fan oven) mark 6. Place flour and fat in a large bowl and rub together until the mixture resembles breadcrumbs. Using a round-bladed knife stir in the cold water a little at a time until the mixture begins to come together. Use your hands to form a ball of pastry. Wrap in clear film and rest for half an hour or so in the fridge.

2. Roll out the pastry and use to line a large, four-hole Yorkshire pudding pan. Prick with a fork or line with foil and fill with baking beans and bake blind for 15 minutes. Allow to cool.

3. To make the filling, peel and core the apples. Cut into generous-sized chunks and place in a pan with a splash of water, the butter, cinnamon and sugar to taste. Gently cook until the edges of each piece just begin to soften. (Don't cook to a mush as the apple will continue to cook in the oven.)

4. Spoon the part-cooked apple into the part-baked pie shells and top with a little more sugar if it tastes very sharp. Cut out four rounds of pastry to top the pies. Press to seal. Make a small slit in the pie crusts and bake for 20-30 minutes, or until the pastry is golden brown and the apple is bubbling.

5. Serve with cold single cream. (Anything like third base?)

Apple Strudel

THE SOUND OF MUSIC (1965)

'Fraulein, is it to be at every meal, or merely at dinnertime, that you intend on leading us all through this rare and wonderful new world of ... indigestion?'

[CAST & CREW]

3 cooking apples
grated rind of 1 lemon
50g (2oz) raisins
50g (2oz) pecans or
  walnuts, chopped
50g (2oz) fresh
  breadcrumbs
75g (3oz) soft brown
  sugar
75g (3oz) ground almonds
$1/2$ tsp cinnamon
3 large sheets filo
  pastry (do not allow to
  dry out)
50g (2oz) butter, melted

Serves 4-6

Now the movie has returned to favour (or am I just getting older?) it's time to bring out the recipe for apple strudel – one of Maria's most favourite things along with 'Cream-coloured ponies'. The recipe for that is over the page. Just kidding!

In the famous song where Maria is rhapsodic in her appreciation of the strudel, she also has the desire to cheer everyone up with lyrics about 'whiskers on kittens'.

I did think about having a recipe for 'Schnitzel and noodles' too, but thought that you would prefer a nice crisp apple strudel instead.

[MISE-EN-SCENE]

1. Peel and core the apples, cut into small dice and place in a bowl. Add the lemon rind, raisins and chopped nuts and stir to combine.

2. In a separate bowl, combine the breadcrumbs, brown sugar, ground almonds and cinnamon. Give this mixture a really good stir.

3. Add 3 tbsp breadcrumb mixture to the apple mixture and stir together.

4. Cover a chopping board with a clean tea towel or clear film. Lay one sheet of pastry on the board and brush liberally with the butter. Repeat with the next two sheets. You don't need to butter the top sheet. You should still have butter left. If not, melt a bit more now.

5. Reserve 1 tbsp breadcrumb mixture. Place one-third of the remaining mixture lengthways down the pastry. Leave space at the ends to allow the pastry to be tucked in before baking.

6. Put half the apple mixture on top. Sprinkle on another third of the breadcrumb mixture, add the remaining apple and then top with the last of the breadcrumb mixture.

7. Butter around the edges of the filo. Tuck the ends in first and press to seal. Lift the edge of the pastry nearest you on top of the apple mixture. Using the tea towel or cling film roll the strudel away from you and the strudel will roll and seal itself.

8. Preheat the oven to 180°C (160°C) mark 5. Slide on to a baking tray. Brush with the remaining butter, sprinkle on the reserved breadcrumbs and bake for 45 minutes.

[VOICE-OVER]

Filo pastry dries out faster than a celebrity in rehab so always keep it covered with a slightly damp tea towel or clear film. It is very delicate so treat with respect.

Baked Beans

BLAZING SADDLES (1974)

'How 'bout some more beans, Mr Taggart?'

[CAST & CREW]

2 x 300g (11oz) cans of
  haricot beans
1 slice belly pork, or 2
  thick rashers smoked
  bacon
1 onion, peeled
4 cloves
4 tsp dark molasses
  sugar
2 tbsp tomato purée
1 tsp English mustard
2 garlic cloves, chopped
several slugs of Tabasco
water
salt and ground black
  pepper
potatoes and cornbread,
  to serve

Serves 4

For the first Hollywood representation of flatulence, Mel Brook's *Blazing Saddles* certainly crafted a tuneful noise! Whether it was a result of the actor's own beans consumption or some clever overdubbing should be left to your imagination, but if they were real, they were brave men to act so close to the naked camp fire flames!

This slow-cooked pork and beans casserole recipe was designed to be left untended in a large cast iron pot over a cooling fire while the cattle were wrangled and the spittoon filled.

If this recipe causes you the same flatulence as Bart, Jim and the boys, you can always blame the dog

[SERVING SUGGESTION]

It is possible to make this using fresh haricot beans when in season, or you could save money by using dried beans. Follow the instructions on the pack very carefully when soaking and boiling dried beans. They are 'windier' (to put it politely) than the tinned version so you will need to balance economy with your desire to keep your friends and relatives in close proximity!

[MISE-EN-SCENE]

1. Pre heat the oven to 140℃ (120℃ fan oven) mark 1. Drain and rinse the haricot beans, then place in a lidded casserole dish.

2. Cut the belly pork or bacon rashers into 2.5cm (1in) pieces and add to the beans.

3. Peel the onion, stud with the cloves and add to the pot.

4. Mix together the sugar, tomato purée, mustard, garlic and Tabasco, then stir in a little water to slacken the sauce and pour over the bean and pork in the casserole.

5. Give the whole thing a good stir to mix and add a little more water to cover if needed. You can add some pepper now if you want but don't add salt as this will toughen the skins of the beans. Cover and bake on a very low heat for 3 hours.

6. Remove the onion and cloves and bake, uncovered, for 1 hour. The sauce will thicken.

7. Season to taste, and serve with potatoes and cornbread.

8. If you feel the beans beginning to take effect, head off into the sunset whistling 'Rawhide' as you go.

Bruce Bogtrotter's Chocolate Cake

MATILDA (1996)

'Miss Trunchbull kept the whole school late because this boy ate some chocolate cake!'

[CAST & CREW]

200g (7oz) butter
200g (7oz) caster sugar
3 large or 4 medium eggs
150g (5oz) plain flour
3 tbsp milk
50g (2oz) cocoa powder
3 tsp baking powder

For the icing:
125g (4oz) butter
75g (3oz) cocoa, sieved
300g (11oz) icing sugar,
  sieved
milk, to slacken the
  mixture

Serves 8

When Bruce Bogtrotter decides to stand up against the evil Miss Trunchbull, he never expected to be eating an entire cake in front of his whole school ... as punishment!

Angry Miss Trunchbull's penalty backfires though when Matilda steps up to encourage Bruce to finish it all to the cheers and jubilation of the whole school.

When you make this massive cake, make sure you share it with your friends. It's what Matilda would want.

[VOICE-OVER]

All manner of sweets can be used to decorate this cake. I favour crushed chocolate flake and marshmallows, but choose your own favourites and indulge. Do not follow Bruce's example and eat the whole thing yourself, unless of course, you are ordered to by Miss Trunchbull.

[MISE-EN-SCENE]

1. Preheat the oven to 180℃ (160℃ fan oven) mark 4. Line a 20cm (8in) loose-bottomed cake tin with baking parchment.

2. Put the butter and sugar in a bowl and beat until pale and fluffy. Beat in 1 egg and 1 tbsp flour. Repeat with the remaining eggs.

3. Stir in the milk and sift in the flour, cocoa and baking powder. Using a metal spoon fold in the dry ingredients until well combined. Pour into the prepared cake tin and bake for 40-45 minutes until a skewer comes out clean when inserted into the middle of the cake. Cool in the tin for 10 minutes, then place on a wire rack until completely cold.

4. To make the icing, melt the butter in a large pan and tip in the cocoa. Cook, stirring for about a minute, then remove from the heat. Beat in the icing sugar. Add the milk, a little at a time, until the icing flows easily. Tip over the cake and allow to cool before decorating.

Chocolate Fondue

WILLY WONKA & THE CHOCOLATE FACTORY (1971)

'Augustus, please don't eat your fingers!'

[CAST & CREW]

200g (8oz) good-quality
  dark chocolate (around
  70% cocoa solids)
150ml (¼ pint) double
  cream
a good slug of liqueur
  or spirit such as
  cointreau, kirsch,
  Malibu, rum
large knob of butter
golden syrup or honey,
  to sweeten
fruit cut into bite-
  sized chunks
marshmallows
amaretti biscuits
anything else you fancy
  dipping into molten
  chocolate
bamboo skewers

Serves 4

Smells are incredibly evocative in this fabulous movie, especially in one of the opening scenes when Charlie stops close to the factory gates and savours the wonderful aromas and sights of the majestic factory. From the look on his face, you understand completely that Wonka's chocolate was what Charlie desired most in the entire world.

When you make this dessert I hope it makes you feel the same. Mind you, as good as this chocolate fondue recipe is, I'd swap it all for a bar of Willy Wonka's Whipple Scrumptious Fudge Mallow Delight!

[VOICE-OVER]

Fruit-based liqueurs work really well in a chocolate fondue. You could also add another dimension to this by using a flavoured chocolate such as chilli or orange.

[MISE-EN-SCENE]

1. Break the chocolate into squares and place in a large heatproof bowl. Pour in the cream and the liqueur or spirit and place over a pan of hot water. (Do not allow the bowl to touch the water or the whole thing will end in disaster.)

2. Stir occasionally until the chocolate has melted and the ingredients combined. Take the bowl off the heat and stir in the butter.

3. Taste the glorious mixture. It may need a little more booze, or even a lot. If you think the fondue needs sweetening add a little golden syrup or honey (sugar will make the mixture gritty).

4. To serve, skewer the fruit and other tasty morsels on to the bamboo sticks, dip, lick and generally enjoy.

5. Anyone who eats a good amount of the fruit should be rewarded with a square or two of good-quality dark chocolate every now and then.

Chocolate Mousse

ROSEMARY'S BABY (1968)

'As long as she ate the mousse, she can't see nor hear. Now sing'

[CAST & CREW]

120ml (4fl oz) double
  cream
120g (4oz) dark
  chocolate (60% cocoa
  solids is best for this
  recipe), broken into
  pieces
25g (1oz) salted butter
4 tsp strong coffee
  (espresso will do
  nicely)
2 eggs, separated
2 tsp soft brown sugar
pinch of salt

Serves 4

Being impregnated with the spawn of the devil probably ranks quite low on the list of things that might happen to you at a suburban dinner party, but happen it does. Sudden deaths, mind games and the solving of an anagram point to a world you wouldn't want to bring a child into ... but Rosemary has no choice.

Hand out this mousse just before the movie starts. If your guests know the plot they might be reluctant to try it. All the more for you then.

[VOICE-OVER]

Adding a little something to this dish might be a good idea although perhaps not the added extra Minnie had in mind. A splash of liqueur, orange zest or finely grated chocolate is fine. Why not finish the dish with a shard of praline? Very professional indeed.

[MISE-EN-SCENE]

1. Pour the cream into a large bowl and whisk to soft peaks. Cover and place in the fridge until needed.

2. Place a heatproof bowl over a pan of barely simmering water and add the chocolate, butter and coffee. Heat until the chocolate has melted. Stir to combine, then remove from the heat and allow to cool slightly. (Don't leave it to set or you will be in a pickle.)

3. Meanwhile, whisk the egg whites with the brown sugar and a pinch of salt, until the whites reach soft-peak stage.

4. Check that the chocolate mixture is cool (as you don't want chocolate scrambled eggs), then beat in the egg yolks using a wooden spoon followed by 1 tbsp egg white to slacken the mixture.

5. Using a metal spoon, fold in alternate large dollops of cream and egg white until all is added and combined. Keep folding gently until no white streaks are visible and the mousse is a uniform chocolate brown.

6. Pour or spoon into serving dishes. Share with friends – and creepy neighbours if you feel brave enough.

Strawberry Chocolate Pie

WAITRESS (2007)

'Vanilla custard with banana. Hold the banana'

[CAST & CREW]

300g (11oz) bourbon or
  Oreo biscuits, crushed
125g (4oz) salted
  butter, melted
1 tbsp golden syrup
300ml (1/2 pint) double
  cream
100ml (31/2 fl oz) milk
3 tsp coffee granules
  (espresso is best)
400g (14oz) dark
  chocolate
2 eggs
250g (10oz) strawberries
ground black pepper

Serves 8

Jenna is a pie genius. She captures moments in her life by naming the pies she makes accordingly.

'I don't want Earl's baby pie' is created when she finds herself unexpectedly pregnant.

'Kick in the pants pie' and 'I hate my husband pie' are very clear in their meaning.

Most transparent of all? 'Pregnant, miserable, self-pitying pie.'

There were a vast number of pies in this film (such as the naughty pumpkin) I could have chosen but instead it was the strawberry chocolate pie that Jenna makes for Old Joe. He looks forward to this

[MISE-EN-SCENE]

1. Preheat oven to 170°C (150°C fan oven) mark 3. Line a 23cm (9in) loose-bottomed flan tin with foil.

2. Place the chocolate biscuits into a roomy bowl. Using the end of a rolling pin, crush the biscuits until they resemble fine breadcrumbs.

3. Melt the butter in a pan with the golden syrup. Pour over the biscuit crumbs and mix well.

4. Tip the mixture into the lined tin and press down well with your fingers or the back of a metal spoon. Refrigerate whilst you make the filling.

5. Put the cream, milk, coffee granules and chocolate in a bowl. Set over a pan of barely simmering water. As the cream heats stir gently until the chocolate has melted and the mixture is smooth and combines. Leave to cool just slightly.

6. Beat the eggs in a separate bowl. Whisk several tablespoons of the warm chocolate mixture into the eggs, then pour into the chocolate cream and combine well. (The cream may thicken slightly as you do this. It's OK!)

7. Take the biscuit base from the fridge. Fill with the chocolate custard and bake for 18-25 minutes until the custard is mostly set and only the middle wobbles when shaken. (Please don't smirk as you read that. It's unbecoming.)

8. Chill the pie, layer with sliced strawberries and grind over a little black pepper. (Trust me.) Serve with cold, cold cream but don't have too much or your fillings will ache.

[VOICE-OVER]

If you want, you could add vanilla extract to the custard when you melt the chocolate. Spiced chocolates would work well too, especially those containing oranges or chilli.

Crème Brûlée

AMELIE (2001)

'Smell that!... Sugarplum, ice cream!'

[CAST & CREW]

4 egg yolks
2¹/₂ tbsp caster sugar
vanilla pod
500ml (18fl oz) double
    cream
5 tbsp granulated sugar

Serves 4

Amelie's over-active imagination allows her mind to wander unhindered from sublime thought to ridiculous assumption.

The pleasure Amelie shares in the cracking of caramel that adorns the top of her crème brûlée is infectious. Amelie decides that her role in life is to bring moments of simple joy into the otherwise mundane lives of those around her.

Make this crème brûlée and you too can gently tap the glassy caramel with the back of your spoon. As the cracks run across the surface, sit back, smile and just enjoy the moment. Amelie would be proud.

[VOICE-OVER]

Crème brûlée is a great dish to make if you have spare egg yolks left from making meringues. You can also depth-charge your custard with soft fruits, especially raspberries, to surprise your guests. Add 2 tbsp cocoa powder to the sugar at the beginning of the recipe to create chocolate crème brûlée. Delicious.

[MISE-EN-SCENE]

1. Preheat the oven to 140°C (120°C fan oven) mark 1. Pop the egg yolks into a large bowl with the sugar and whisk together until pale and fluffy.

2. Split the vanilla pod lengthways and scrape out the gooey seeds with the point of your knife. Then put the whole lot into a large pan. Add the double cream and slowly heat until the cream begins to make tiny bubbles at the edge. Remove the pan from the heat and allow to cool a little.

3. Whisking as you pour, add the warm cream to the eggy sugary foam. (The whisking is vital otherwise you will have sweet scrambled eggs in your bowl rather than the beginnings of custard.)

4. Pour the mixture back into the pan and stir until thickened. Pour the custard into four ramekins to about three-quarters full, then arrange in a large baking dish. Pour hot water around the ramekins to about 2.5cm (1in) deep.

5. Bake for 30 minutes until just set. Remove from the oven and cool.

6. When cool sprinkle the custards with sugar and flash under a very hot grill until the sugar melts. If you are feeling flamboyant, use a blowtorch to impress your guests. (I cheat and make a caramel by melting the sugar in a pan and pouring it over the custard. It guarantees the all-important layer of crisp caramel.

[CAST & CREW]

rind of 1 lemon
250g (9oz) plain flour
125g (4oz) butter,
  margarine, lard, or a
  combination
4-6 tbsp ice-cold water
250ml (9fl oz) double
  cream, plus extra to
  serve
2 eggs
2 tbsp caster sugar
nutmeg

Serves 4

This infamous custard pie fight – in *Battle of the Century* – is the largest in cinematic history. 3000 actual custard pies are thrown, squashed, slipped on and sat in. Why? Well, Stan and Ollie are attempting to claim on an insurance policy but, of course, fail miserably. When a banana skin fails to injure Stan sufficiently to claim on their insurance, they decide to bring in the pies.

Before you make this gorgeous pie, draw up a list of people in your life who really annoy you. I'm not encouraging you to throw it at them but you could take the opportunity to work out your differences over a slice and a cup of tea. Of course, if that doesn't work, then be prepared to duck!

[VOICE-OVER]

The Los Angeles Pie Company who made all the pies for filming did so in just one day. That's a whole load of pie! If you need to make lots of pies in a hurry you could always use ready-made pastry or even pastry shells. If you do that, choose unsweetened ones. It makes the filling taste even sweeter.

[MISE-EN-SCENE]

1. Preheat oven to 190°C (170°C fan oven) mark 5.

2. Sift the flour into a roomy bowl and rub in the fat until the mixture resembles breadcrumbs. Using a round-bladed knife stir in the ice-cold water a little at a time until the dough begins to come together.

3. Using your hands very gently bring the dough together in a ball. Wrap in clear film and leave to rest in the refrigerator for at least 30 minutes.

4. Roll out the dough and line a 15cm (6in) flan dish. Prick with a fork or line with foil and fill with baking beans and bake blind for 15 minutes. Allow to cool. Reduce the oven temperature to 180°C (160°C fan oven) mark 4.

5. Put the lemon rind in a pan with the double cream and heat slowly to about blood temperature. Remove from the heat.

6. In a separate bowl whisk together the eggs and the sugar. When thoroughly combined, pour in the lemony cream and whisk together well. Strain into the partly baked pastry case and discard the lemon peel.

7. Grate a little nutmeg over the surface of the custard and bake for 30-40 minutes until only the centre of the pie gives a little wobble. Allow to cool and serve with ice-cold fresh cream.

Jelly

9¹/₂ WEEKS (1986)

'Every time I see you, you're buying a chicken'

[CAST & CREW]

200g (7oz) soft fruit
  (such as strawberries,
  blackberries,
  raspberries and
  tayberries)
1-2 tbsp caster sugar
3 leaves of gelatin
water or elderflower
  cordial

Serves 2

Let's not be coy about this, the reason many of us went to see *9¹/₂ Weeks* in the first instance was because of its notoriety. The level of nudity and sexually charged scenes, however well-shot, were what got us through the door.

  Yes, there were a lot of sex scenes, but for us foodies, there was also a lot of food! In the classic scene, when the buffet starts to be removed from the fridge, you know only too well that John (Mickey Rourke) isn't packing for a picnic. Food porn in both senses of the word fills the screen.

[VOICE-OVER]

This jelly tastes even better when served with ice-cold cream or really good vanilla ice cream. Or you could follow Elizabeth and John's example by serving your jelly with cold pasta, maraschino cherries, fresh strawberries, black olives, cherry tomatoes, fizzy water, green chillies, a glass of milk and a jar of honey. In this instance, I'd suggest making sure the floor has a wipe-clean surface!

[MISE-EN-SCENE]

1. Taste the fruits to check their tartness, then place in a large bowl and sprinkle over the sugar according to your own judgement.

2. Cover the bowl with clear film. Zap the fruit in the microwave for 20 seconds at a time until the fruit is warm, then stir and leave for half an hour. Alternatively, place the bowl over a pan of warm water for half an hour to encourage the juices to flow.

3. Place a clean tea towel or new J cloth into a colander or large sieve. Pour in the fruit and the juices and leave to drip overnight. (Don't be tempted to push the fruit through, this will make your jelly cloudy. Not that Mickey Rourke would mind, but it matters to me!)

4. Pour the juice into a measuring jug and make up to 500ml (18fl oz) with water or a diluted cordial.

5. Pour a little of the juice into a mug and add the gelatine sheets into this liquid. (You can break them up if you want to.) Allow the gelatine sheets to swell then place the mug in a pan of hot water until the gelatine melts. Stir in the remaining juice and pour into a 500ml (18fl oz) jelly mould. Leave to set for 4-6 hours.

'*Joe, we can't go running around town with a hot princess!*'

[CAST & CREW]

285ml (10fl oz) single
  cream
1 vanilla pod or 1 tsp
  good-quality vanilla
  extract
4 egg yolks
125g (4oz) caster sugar
50ml (2fl oz) limoncello
  or similar citrus
  liqueur
285ml (10fl oz) double
  cream
100g (3^1/$_2$ oz) dark
  chocolate

Serves 4-6

Doing the right thing is a central theme of *Roman Holiday*. Gregory Peck's Joe does the right thing by the Princess when he returns her treasured photographs and promises to keep her secret. The Princess puts duty to her country above her desire to stay with the man she has fallen in love with.

You will need to do the right thing too. When the movie has finished, sniff back any sorrow, open the freezer door, find this bowl of ice cream that you had made earlier and bury your sadness in a bowlful of rich, tasty gelato. There, don't we all feel better now?

[VOICE-OVER]

Save the egg whites for another day. You can freeze them very successfully. When you are ready, defrost them and make meringues or macaroons.

[MISE-EN-SCENE]

1. Put the single cream and vanilla pod (split lengthways) or vanilla extract in a pan, and heat gently until the cream begins to bubble around the edge. Remove from the heat and cool a little.

2. Whisk together the egg yolks and sugar until pale and foamy. Add the slightly cooled cream to the egg mixture, stirring all the time. When combined strain back into the pan. Heat very gently, stirring continuously until the custard thickens. Remove from the heat. Add in the liqueur and stir again. Leave to cool and then chill for at least 1 hour.

3. Whisk the double cream until it forms soft peaks. Using a spatula, fold in the cooled custard, then churn using an ice cream machine until set. (If you don't have an ice cream maker, pour into a large plastic container and freeze for 1 hour. Whisk up with a fork and re-freeze. Continue like this until the ice cream is set. This may take up to 3 hours.)

4. Melt the chocolate and drizzle over the surface of the ice cream. Leave to re-set. Serve in a waffle cone with the sound and smell of Vespas careering dangerously in and out of ancient ruins in the background.

Pecan Pie

HAIRSPRAY (2008)

'I've tasted chocolate, and I'm never goin' back!'

[CAST & CREW]

100g (3¹/₂ oz) soft brown
  sugar (dark or light
  depending how treacly
  you like things)
40g (1¹/₂ oz) butter
2 tbsp golden syrup
pinch of salt
a few drops of vanilla
  extract
2 tbsp rum, whisky or
  tequila
2 eggs
1–2 tsp single cream
125g (4oz) pecan halves
15cm (6in) blind baked
  pastry case
cream or ice cream, to
  serve

Serves 4

Food, along with music and dance, is at the heart of
Hairspray. And lots of it too.

What Edna lacks in attitude, motormouth Maybelle
has in bucket loads, and she also has vast quantities
of food. Edna can't go home without sampling
Maybelle's feast and once she begins to eat she is
hooked! Slices of ham, chocolate swirls and hogs head
cheese tempt Edna out into the open after years as a
recluse. Once her spirit is woken though there is no
stopping this woman! Amen.

[VOICE-OVER]

Chopped pecans will work fine in the mixture but get a few whole ones for the top of the pie too!

[MISE-EN-SCENE]

1. Preheat the oven to 180℃ (160℃ fan oven) mark 4.

2. Put the sugar, butter and syrup in a pan and heat gently to melt. Add the salt, vanilla extract and spirit of your choice. Bring to the boil, stirring. Once boiling stir the mixture constantly and boil for 1 minute. (The mixture will 'soufflé' and rise up as it boils. Just keep stirring.)

3. Leave the mixture to cool and thicken slightly. Meanwhile, whisk the eggs and cream in a separate bowl until the mixture becomes pale and light in texture.

4. Combine the egg and the syrup mixtures and whisk until well incorporated. Reserve about 25g (1oz) of the pecan halves for decoration, then stir in the remaining nuts until covered with the sticky mixture.

5. Pour the mixture into the pastry case and decorate with the remaining pecan halves. Bake for 35-40 minutes until set and well risen.

6. Lacquer your hair up high, put on your dancing shoes and dig in to this pecan pie. Ice cream or cold pouring cream is an essential addition. Low-fat versions are NOT acceptable.

Mash

M*A*S*H* (1970)

'Well, what's the slop du jour?'

[CAST & CREW]

500g (17 oz) small
  floury potatoes
100g (3 1/2oz) butter
125 ml (4fl oz) milk
  warmed
salt
pepper
potato ricer or masher

Serves 2

Mash. Quite simply the greatest of all comfort foods. It goes brilliantly with liver and onions as well as some decent sausages and a mug-full of rich gravy – maybe even the odd root vegetable too. Did you know that mash also happens to be named after this movie. No, that isn't true. I'm just checking to see if you lot are still reading this preamble or have just dived straight into the recipe of this beloved dish.
  Mash, like the movie and the US TV series of the same name, is simple but always very fulfilling.

[VOICE-OVER]

If the quartermaster hasn't been able to source potatoes you can always make a sweet potato mash or eke out the potatoes with carrots, parsnips or other root vegetables. Variations on mashed potato are endless but can include the addition of: olive oil instead of butter, olives or tapenade, pesto, soured cream and chives, spring onions, fried onions, wholegrain mustard, garlic, sweet potato, carrots etc. etc. etc. Go on, be adventurous.

[MISE-EN-SCENE]

1. Boil the potatoes in their skins until soft. Testing the softness with the point of a knife is the easiest way to do this. When cooked, drain and allow to steam in their skins for five minutes to allow any excess moisture to evaporate.

2. Peel the cooked potatoes and using a potato ricer rice them into the pan. If you don't have a potato ricer then mash them with a masher.

3. Tip in the milk and half of the butter. The milk must be warm or the starches in the potato will become gluey and the mash will cool down.

4. Using a wooden spoon beat well. Taste and season the mash. The dish should be smooth and lump free.

5. Serve in a large dish, make a well in the top of the mashed potato and place the last of the butter in the well to melt into a golden pool. A food for sharing and a real taste of home.

6. If you don't like the look of anything else from the mess tent just stir in a large handful of grated cheese. Return to your bunk and hope for a quiet night.

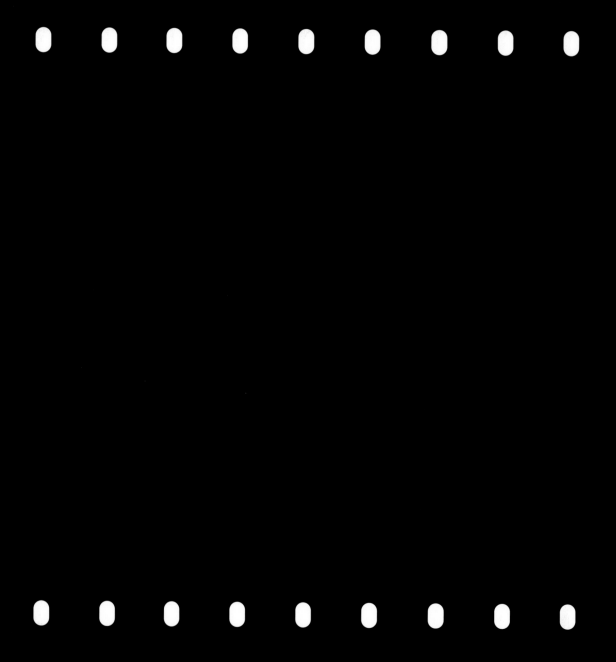

Out-takes

OK, so you're probably stuffed.
But here are some more delicious dinners, just in case
your eyes are bigger than your belly.

Cherryade Chocolate Float

GREASE (1978)

*'Uh, I'm not very hungry; just give me a double Polar Burger wit'
everything and a cherry soda wit' chocolate ice cream'*

[CAST & CREW]

4 glacé cherries
2 tall knickerbocker
  glory glasses
1 large bottle
  cherryade, well-chilled
several scoops chocolate
  ice cream
4 long straws
2 long spoons
chocolate flakes

Serves 2

Both the T-birds and the Pink Ladies find the menu at
Violet's Frosty Palace offers exactly what their
developing palates crave. Burgers, chips, ice cream
sundaes and artificially coloured, sugar-laden
milkshakes are all ordered and find their way out of
the kitchen and towards the gangs.

Danny's order of Polar Burger, cherry soda and
chocolate ice cream on his first date with Sandy
pretty much sums up his, and most teenage boys,
diets.

Though how they dance and sing so energetically
afterwards – and not throw up – is beyond me.

[VOICE-OVER]

A twist on a classic ice cream soda, this drink looks incredible. You could make the balls of ice cream ahead of time and return them to the freezer on a baking sheet until needed. This will save you time when making up the floats.

[MISE-EN-SCENE]

1. Pop a couple of glacé cherries in the bottom of each glass.

2. Fill the glasses two-thirds-full with the cherryade.

3. Take a scoop of chocolate ice cream and slide gently into the cherryade. It will fizz and resemble something slightly satanic but this is why it is really important not to overfill the glasses initially.

4. Add two straws and a spoon to each glass, then decorate with a chocolate flake.

5. After drinking, sit still until the drink has gone down. Once it has, run around frantically to get the sugar out of your system as soon as possible.

Chicken Salad Sandwich

FIVE EASY PIECES (1970)

'Now all you have to do is hold the chicken, bring me the toast, give me a check for the chicken salad sandwich, and you haven't broken any rules'

[CAST & CREW]

2 slices wheat bread, toasted (not an English muffin or a coffee roll)

butter, at room temperature for spreading

mayonnaise, for spreading

several lettuce leaves

chicken breast, cooked and shredded

salt and ground black pepper

Serves 1

In need of sustenance during a journey back home to visit his sick father, Bobby finds that the waitress in the diner they stop at hasn't heard the maxim that the customer is always right.

Bobby only wants plain toast and an omelette but when he discovers that not only do they have bread *and a* toaster – but he can't have toast – he becomes confused. The waitress is adamant that there are no deviations from the menu. Bobby's response to the waitress's 'You want me to hold the chicken, huh?' has got to be one of the best pieces of lateral thinking caught on camera:

'I want you to hold it between your knees.'

[VOICE-OVER]

Toasted bread is a good choice for sandwiches where the filling is quite damp. It provides a little more resistance and prevents the sandwich contents from ending up in your lap too quickly. If you don't like butter, mayonnaise is a good way to seal the bread and this too stops filling-seepage!

[MISE-EN-SCENE]

1. Remember, the customer is always right.

2. Allow the toast to cool slightly, then spread one piece with butter and the other with mayonnaise.

3. Lay several leaves of lettuce on the buttered toast. Season with salt only.

4. Top the lettuce with the shredded chicken breast. Make sure the chicken covers the bread evenly. Season with freshly ground black pepper.

5. Place the toast, mayonnaise side down, on top of the chicken.

6. Cut into two pieces. You may wish to accompany this with a large side of rudeness and sarcasm.

7. For toast follow the above instructions but stop at point 3.

'This is my man, this is my restaurant, and you two are gonna turn around and walk right out of here – without your dry white toast, without your four fried chickens, and without Matt "Guitar" Murphy!'

[CAST & CREW]

8 chicken pieces
  (thighs, drumsticks or
  breast portions)
250g (9oz) carton
  buttermilk
Tabasco, to taste
8 tbsp plain flour
smoked paprika (or your
  own preferred spice
  mix), to season
vegetable shortening or
  oil, for frying
salt and ground black
  pepper
greens, mashed potatoes
  and onion rings, to
  serve

Serves 1 or more

Jake and Elwood Blues take the biscuit when it comes to bizarre eating. Two scenes in this classic movie famously occur in restaurants and the Brothers' eating habits, while always outrageous, are also terrific.

Even if Aretha's 'R.E.S.P.E.C.T' doesn't scare 'Guitar' Murphy as much as she hoped, Elwood, at least, gets some toast – one of the few moments when the brothers take a brief break from all that law-breaking and carnage.

[VOICE-OVER]

You might find it cheaper to portion a whole chicken rather than buy pieces. Using kitchen shears cut along one side of the backbone and then repeat for the other side. Remove the leg portions, and cut the breast section in two. Easy!

[DRY WHITE TOAST]

I'm sure Elwood wouldn't mind if you just stuck a few slices of white bread in a toaster!

[MISE-EN-SCENE]

1. Take each chicken piece, wash and pat dry, then season with salt and pepper.

2. Pour the buttermilk into a plastic container and add a few splashes of Tabasco to your taste.

3. Mix in the chicken pieces, cover with clear film and pop in the fridge for between two and ten hours. Overnight is fine too.

4. Put the flour in a plastic food bag and season well with paprika or your chosen spice mix. Remove the chicken pieces from the marinade and place in the flour-filled bag. Shake well.

5. Heat 1cm ($\frac{1}{2}$ in) oil or shortening in a heavy-based frying pan or skillet.

6. Lower the chicken pieces into the fat and cook for about 20 minutes. Drain well and serve with greens, mash and onion rings. A side of fried green tomatoes and gravy would be good too.

Fried Green Tomatoes

FRIED GREEN TOMATOES (1991)

'Oh, what I wouldn't give for a plate of fried green tomatoes like we used to have at the café'

[CAST & CREW]

6 large green tomatoes
Dripping, vegetable oil
  or the fat left in the
  pan after you've fried
  some rashers of bacon
Cornmeal (fine or
  medium), for coating
salt and ground black
  pepper
bacon, eggs and home
  fries, to serve

Serves 2

Read what you will into the closeness of the relationship between Evelyn and Ninny, but it's their love of the food they serve at the Whistle Stop Café that reflects their roots.

Every scrap and morsel of food is used on the menu as it is too precious to waste, even the rock-hard, still-green tomatoes that have little hope of ever ripening. Ruth and Idgie take this unloved fruit and turn it into something really quite spectacular.

But one word of advice, should you ever find yourself at the Whistle Stop Café, don't order the ribs.

[VOICE-OVER]

The fat for cooking this dish is important. It really needs some taste of its own to enhance the tomatoes. Use vegetable oil if you have to, but drippings from a Sunday roast would be better. Fat from frying bacon is even better. This is not a dish for vegetarians even if it contains vegetables.

You can keep dripping in the fridge until you need it. Save in a covered pot or tub. If you have not used within a week, throw away. This scenario should never occur, because you can always use it up making fried bread. A shake of Worcester sauce over the fried bread livens it up no end.

[MISE-EN-SCENE]

1. Slice the tomatoes into 1cm ($1/2$ in) thick rounds. Lay on a plate and season with salt and a few grinds of black pepper.

2. Heat the fat in a frying pan. Dip the tomatoes in the cornmeal, coating well on both sides.

3. Fry the fat for 2-3 minutes on each side. They should be crispy on the outside and soft in the middle.

4. Serve with crispy bacon, eggs, home fries, and an appointment with a cardiologist.

[CAST & CREW]

butter, for frying
1 small onion, finely
  diced
3 large eggs
splash of milk
pinch of salt
oil, for frying
$1/2$ green pepper,
  seeded and sliced
handful of button
  mushrooms, halved
handful of strong
  cheese, grated

Serves 1 (as a main)
Serves 2 (as a snack)

Harry Palmer (Michael Caine) is no James Bond. In order to seduce women, Harry has to embrace his feminine side and cook. Fortunately for Harry, the film's writer, Len Deighton, was also a renowned foodie. Len helped Michael Caine to rehearse the recipe and it's his hand you see in the egg-cracking scene.

The producer of the movie wasn't happy when he saw the cooking scene

as he was worried the audience would assume that Harry was gay. Only when Michael Caine protested that the intended seduction was of a woman did he grudgingly relent. It's a good job too – omelettes became the new way to impress the love of your life.

[VOICE-OVER]

A stringy cheese, such as fontina or gruyère, work beautifully well in an omelette, especially with a few scraps of decent ham. Chop up a fiery chilli too if you want to add a bit of heat.

[MISE-EN-SCENE]

1. Prepare your ingredients and arrange them close by. This will not only make your kitchen look like the set of a cookery programme, but once the eggs begin to cook speed is of the essence.

2. Heat a knob of butter in a pan and sauté the onion for about 5 minutes until translucent, then remove and set aside.

3. Break the eggs into a bowl. (If you want to do this one-handed, you will need to practise, practise, practise.) Add a splash of milk and pinch of salt, then whisk until light and airy.

4. Heat a splash of oil and a knob of butter in the pan. Add the egg and leave for one minute. Using a spatula, pull the set egg from the edge of the pan to the middle. Tip the pan to allow the egg to cover the pan.

5. Quickly scatter over the pepper, mushrooms and onions, then the cheese.

6. While there is still a little liquid egg visible on the surface, remove from the heat.

7. Slide the half of the omelette onto a plate and then fold the remaining half on top, encasing the filling.

8. Serve to someone who looks willing to be seduced or just make it for yourself and eat while watching a decent spy movie.

Bhajis and Pakora

BEND IT LIKE BECKHAM (2002)

'The offside rule is when the French mustard has to be between the teriyaki sauce and the sea salt'

[CAST & CREW]

4 heaped tbsp gram (chickpea) flour (plain flour will do if you can't find gram flour)
$^1/_2$ tsp salt
$^1/_2$ tsp chilli powder
1 tsp cumin seeds, bruised
1 tsp coriander seeds, crushed
green chilli, finely diced (optional)
1 large onion, halved and thinly sliced
4 small cauliflower florets
1 potato or sweet potato
$^1/_2$ green pepper, seeded and sliced
8 spinach leaves
water, to mix
oil, for deep frying
mint yogurt raita and chutneys of your choice, to serve
Serves 4

Jess finds that, despite ambition and great natural ability, her decision to become a footballer doesn't make her popular. Her frustrated family simply cannot understand why she prefers running round muddy fields to staying in a warm kitchen making classic Indian dishes. I agree!

Spicy bhajis and pakora are staple snacks in both Indian restaurants and homes across the land and are incredibly fun to make. There's even a section on the film's DVD where Jess's aunts tell you how to make other classic Indian dishes such as aloo gobi. Check it out!

[VOICE-OVER]

Use the chutneys to give the pakora fire and heat especially if children are eating this dish too. Less brave souls should go for sweet mango chutney but also include a lime pickle for the fearless.

[MISE-EN-SCENE]

1. Peel the potato and cut into 5mm ($^1/_4$ in) slices. Place in a pan and cover with cold water. Bring to the boil, then reduce heat and simmer for 4-5 minutes. Drain well and set aside.

2. Spoon the flour into a large bowl and add the salt, spices and fresh chilli, if using. Mix well to combine.

3. Gradually stir in enough water to make a batter the consistency of thick double cream, then leave to stand for a moment or two. If the mixture thickens too much add a little more water.

4. Divide the mixture into two bowls. Add the sliced onion to one bowl and give it a good stir.

5. Heat a good amount of oil in a deep pan and heat to 180°C. Drop spoonfuls of the onion mixture into the oil and cook until golden and crispy. Remove and drain on kitchen paper. Dip the vegetables into the second bowl of batter and fry in the same way until golden and crispy.

6. Serve with a mint yogurt raita and chutneys of your choice.

Turkish Delight

THE LION, THE WITCH AND THE WARDROBE (2005)

'You've been sneaking second helpings, haven't you?'

[CAST & CREW]

2 tsp lemon juice
400g (14oz) sugar
$^1/_2$ tsp cream of tartar
100g (3$^1/_2$ oz) cornflour
1 tbsp rosewater
handful of pistachios,
  slithered (optional)
1 heaped tbsp candied
  peel or candied ginger,
  finely chopped
  (optional)
75g (3oz) icing sugar

**Makes 36 pieces (just
enough to feed a family
of Beavers and Fauns!)**

No one is ever ambivalent towards Turkish Delight –
you either love it or hate it.

The White Witch must have been glad that Edmund was
a lover and not a hater. When she plies him with
magical Turkish Delight he becomes a pawn instantly
under her devious control, willing to offer up even
his siblings in return for one more taste of its
sweet stickiness.

In her quest to rid Narnia of the sons of Adam and
the daughters of Eve, the White Witch's powers are a
real advantage as she magically conjures up pre-made
Turkish Delight. In truth, making it is a bit of a
palaver. But if you're after a sweet to make your
teeth ache then this is the recipe for you.

[MISE-EN-SCENE]

1. Lightly oil a 12x12cm (5x5in) square cake tin. Line with baking parchment and lightly oil that too.

2. Put the lemon juice, caster sugar and 175ml (6fl oz) water in a heavy-based pan. Stir and bring to the boil. Keep heating gently until the syrup reaches the soft-ball stage. (When you drop a little into a bowl of cold water it should form a soft ball.) Remove from the heat.

3. In a second pan combine 300ml ($^1/_2$ pint) water, the cream of tartar and 75g (3oz) of the cornflour. Stir really well and keep stirring as you heat the mixture. Whisk until smooth. (It will be very gelatinous at this stage. Do not panic.)

4. Whisk in the lemon syrup and bring back to a simmer. Simmer gently for 45 minutes to 1 hour, stirring every 5 minutes or so.

5. When it is almost too stiff to whisk, remove from the heat and add your choice of flavourings. Rosewater is very traditional but tends to taste like old ladies' perfume. Pistachios are another lovely addition, as is candied peel. If you like it spicy, add some crystallised ginger.

6. Pour the mixture into the oiled container and leave to cool for at least 4 hours.

7. Mix together the icing sugar and remaining cornflour. Dust a little over the work surface. Turn out the Turkish Delight and slice into bite-size pieces. Turn them over in the powder and store. Eat within 48 hours of making. (Not because of magic but because they begin to change back into their component parts!)

[VOICE-OVER]

Rolling Turkish delight in toasted coconut is another traditional way to serve this sweet.

Wafer-thin Mints

MONTY PYTHON'S MEANING OF LIFE (1983)

'Better get a bucket. I'm gonna throw up!'

[CAST & CREW]

1 small egg white
350g (12oz) icing sugar,
  sifted
peppermint extract, to
  taste
100g (4oz) dark
  chocolate (minimum 70%
  cocoa solids), melted

Makes about 35-40

We've all been to a dinner party where at the end of a lovely meal, when you are stuffed to the gills, the kind host offers everyone 'coffee ... and a waffer-thin mint?' and everyone in the room laughs hysterically at the thought of Mr Creosote exploding everywhere ... and on everyone.

Having one of these melt in the mouth mints is a good way to round off a big meal and cleanse the palete ... assuming you all have space for the added volume.

I have included a dark chocolate coating on my version. I am sure Mr Creosote wouldn't have refused the gilding of the lily, as it were. Waffer!

[VOICE-OVER]

These little mints can be cut into different shapes, or dipped in egg white and sugar to give them a crystallised finish, or even coloured with a few drops of green food colouring. They are best served with a cup of good, strong coffee. Access to a vomitorium is optional.

[MISE-EN-SCENE]

1. In a very clean, grease-free bowl, whisk the egg white until light and foamy. Add a capful of peppermint extract and whisk again.

2. Tip half of the icing sugar into the egg white and, using the whisk, mix very well. Taste and add more peppermint flavour if you wish.

3. Add half the remaining icing sugar and, using your hands, knead together to form a very stiff paste. Continue adding icing sugar until you have a smooth ball of dough that is neither too sticky nor too crumbly. It should have an almost silky feel when rolled into a ball.

4. Cut the ball in two. Keep one covered with clear film and place the other half between two sheets of parchment paper. Roll the paste out to about 3mm ($1/8$ in) thick. Peel off the top sheet of paper and cut into 2x4cm ($3/4$ x $1 1/2$ in) rectangles. Lift off the bottom sheet of paper and place on a wire rack to dry. Repeat with the remaining peppermint paste. Leave to dry for about 12 hours or overnight.

5. Dip each wafer-thin mint in melted chocolate and leave to set on a sheet of greaseproof paper. (Try hard not to lick your fingers as you go otherwise this gets very sticky, not to mention being unhygienic.)

6. Think very carefully before offering these to anyone who mentions feeling very full.

The World's Best Sandwich

SPANGLISH (2004)

'Just do it or I'll light my hair on fire and start punching myself in the face!'

[CAST & CREW]

2 thick slices fresh
  brown bread (preferably
  from a baker rather
  than the supermarket)
mayonnaise, for
  spreading
4 rashers streaky bacon
strong hard cheese (such
  as Monterey Jack),
  grated or sliced
1 tomato, sliced
a few round lettuce
  leaves (iceberg will
  not do)
butter, for frying
1 egg

Serves 1

Adam Sandler's character in *Spanglish* takes an iconic American BLT sandwich and, with a few professional tweaks, transforms it into something that has the entire cinema audience drooling into their laps.

For a movie about a chef, you might have expected more food on show but the film is much more about the characters and their relationships with one another and how they all try to succeed in achieving their personal goals.

If your goal is to simply eat the world's best sandwich, then try this recipe. You certainly won't be disappointed. If you happen to be a vegetarian, then leave out the bacon and substitute avocado instead.

[VOICE-OVER]

The sandwich was created for the movie by Thomas Keller of The French Laundry. The DVD extras even show Keller teaching Sandler how to make this sandwich for the first time, so take a look if you need some extra hints.

[MISE-EN-SCENE]

1. Put on your pinny and imagine you are Thomas Keller.

2. Put the bread in a toaster and toast lightly. Remove and lay on a large plate. Spread one slice with mayonnaise.

3. Grill the bacon until crispy, then drain on kitchen towels.

4. Arrange the cheese on the remaining plain slice of toast and return to the grill. Watch like a hawk as you want the cheese to melt but not colour or bubble.

5. Carefully lay the bacon on the mayonnaised toast. (Keller was insistent that you should make sure the meat is evenly distributed.) Top with the sliced tomato and the lettuce.

6. Melt a knob of butter in a non-stick frying pan. Fry the egg gently, flip to ensure that the top is cooked but the yolk must remain runny. Slide the egg on to the lettuce.

7. Crown the sandwich with the cheesey toast. Slice in half allowing the golden yolk to drip over the rest of the sandwich filling.

8. Open a cold beer and enjoy The World's Best Sandwich.

GHOSTBUSTERS (1984)

'Well, let's say this Twinkie represents the normal amount of psychokinetic energy in the New York area. Based on this morning's sample, it would be a Twinkie thirty-five feet long, weighing approximately six hundred pounds'

[CAST & CREW]

100g (3^1/$_2$ oz) butter, at
  room temperature
200g (7oz) caster sugar
1 tsp vanilla extract
2 eggs
150g (5oz) self-raising
  flour
^{1}/$_2$ tsp salt
^{1}/$_2$ tbsp baking powder
125ml (4fl oz) milk
flavourless oil, for
  greasing

For the filling:
1^1/$_4$ tsp plain flour
100ml (3^1/$_2$ fl oz) milk
70g (3oz) butter, at
  room temperature
1 tsp vanilla extract

Makes 9

This recipe isn't for the super-sized twinkie as described by Egon Spengler, mere moments before Manhattan is plunged into paranormal darkness, but a more 'normal' bite-size one, perfect to share with fellow fans of this supernatural comedy.

Just be careful with the creamy filling — as Dr Pete Venkmen might say — you wouldn't want to get 'slimed' during the film's scarier bits.

[MISE-EN-SCENE]

1. Preheat the oven to 180℃ (160℃ fan oven) mark 4.

2. Place the butter and sugar in a bowl and beat together using an electric whisk until the mixture becomes pale and light in texture.

3. Add the vanilla extract and whisk in the eggs one at a time.

4. In a separate bowl, sift together the flour, salt and baking powder.

5. Fold in a little of the flour, followed by a little of the milk, and continue to fold in the ingredients in this way, ending with the last few spoonfuls of flour. (Be careful not to knock too much air out of the mixture while folding the ingredients together.)

6. Lightly grease a nine-hole mini loaf tin. Spoon the mixture into each loaf tin to about two-thirds full. (If you have any leftover mixture, spoon into cupcake cases and bake for 15 minutes until golden and risen.)

7. Bake the mini loaves for 15 minutes until golden brown. A toothpick, inserted into the middle of the cake, should come out clean. Leave to cool in the tin.

8. Meanwhile, make the filling. Put the flour in a small bowl, add a splash of the milk and mix to a smooth paste. Gradually stir in the rest of the milk, then pour into a small pan. Heat gently, stirring constantly, until the mixture begins to bubble. Continuing to stir, simmer gently for three minutes.

Remove from the heat and set aside to cool.

9. In a separate bowl, beat the butter and sugar until creamy and pale, then beat into the cooled milk mixture using an electric hand mixer. Beat in the vanilla and continue beating until the mixture is light and airy. Shop-bought Twinkies are filled using a three-syringed injection tube. For this home-made version, slice the top off each mini loaf, then scoop out a little of the inside to form a well. Spoon or pipe the filling into the well and replace the top.

10. Who ya gonna call?

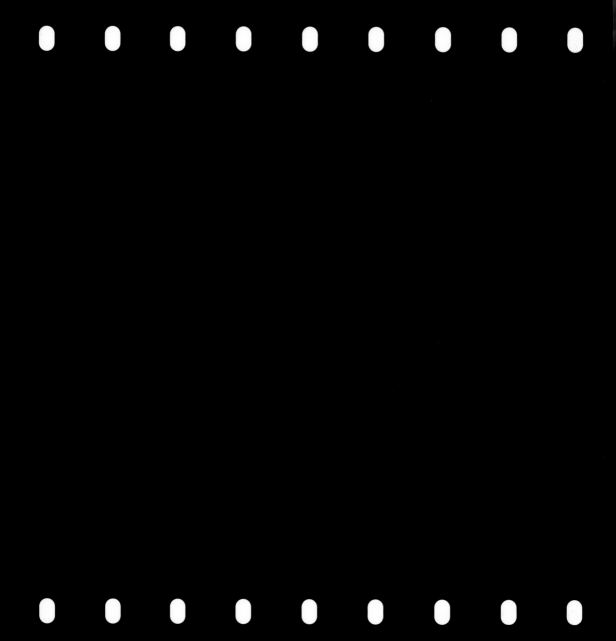

TV Dinners

Trays at the ready? TV on loud? Then press play
for your final course of delicious dinners...

Donuts

THE SIMPSONS (1989-PRESENT)

'Donuts.Is there anything they can't do?'

[CAST & CREW]

180ml (6fl oz) warm milk
60ml (2 $^1/_4$fl oz) warm
  water
1 tsp granulated sugar
2 tsp dried yeast
425g (15oz) plain flour
$^1/_2$ tsp salt
1 egg
1 tsp vanilla extract
vegetable oil, for
  deep-frying

**Makes 8-12 (depending on
thickness, and I'm not
talking about Homer!)**

Homer Simpson is not a
complicated man. Food,
Duff, TV and his family
are the most important
things in his life. And
I think he would agree
that they come in that
order too.

Homer regards donuts as
an essential food group
and it's very rare that
we see him without one.

Balancing his 'diet'
with a donut in one hand
and a beer in the other
keeps Homer the fine
figure of a man we have all come to love and adore.

If you don't want to end up with Homer's physique
then I suggest you keep these, admittedly tasty,
donuts as an occasional treat. Doh!

[MISE-EN-SCENE]

1. Put down the TV remote control, raise yourself slowly up from the sofa, step over Santa's Little Helper and make your way to the kitchen. Ask for directions or a map if needed.

2. Pour the milk into a small pan and warm through until just lukewarm. Tip into a jug, add the warm water and stir in the sugar.

3. Whisk in the dried yeast and leave for ten minutes or so for the yeast to activate and start foaming.

4. Put the flour into the large bowl of a kitchen mixer (or bowl) and add the salt.

5. Once the yeast has activated and left foam on the surface of the liquid, whisk in the egg and the vanilla extract.

6. Attach a dough hook to the mixer; pour the liquids into the dry ingredients and leave to combine for 2-3 minutes. If you are using a bowl, make your hands into a claw shape and combine the ingredients using a circular movement. Once amalgamated you will need to continue to work this very loose batter for another five minutes. This is hard work but remember the reward is hot donuts! Cover with clear film or a clean tea towel and leave to rise for 1 hour in a warm place.

7. Tip the risen dough on to a floured surface and pat out. Roll to a thickness of about 1cm (1/2 in) and cut out. In homage to Homer, I use a pint glass for the outer round and a shot glass for the inner hole.

8. Leave to rise for a further 30 minutes. Heat 5cm (2in) vegetable oil in a deep pan. Fry the donuts on one side until golden, flip over and fry on the other side. They will puff up as they fry. Drain on kitchen paper. Allow to cool slightly before eating.

[VOICE-OVER]

Donuts need little embellishment when very fresh. Homer prefers his iced with sprinkles but you must allow the donuts to cool before you do this. A simple glacé icing and a tub of hundreds and thousands will do the job. For a hot donut, a tumble in caster sugar is usually enough.

Chef's Chocolate Salty Balls

SOUTH PARK (1997-PRESENT)

'Oh! Suck on my chocolate salty balls, put 'em in your mouth and suck 'em'

[CAST & CREW]

400g (14oz) dark
  chocolate
2 tbsp strong black
  coffee
1 small can of condensed
  milk toffee
cocoa powder, for
  coating
sea salt, for coating

Makes 40-50 balls

Chef is generally one of the more mature and respected adults in *South Park* but, despite this, he still manages to bring every conversation he has with Stan, Eric, Kenny and Cartman round to the topic of sex - something these children should really have no idea about.

Not wanting to shy away from the chance to indulge in the Chef's kind offer (check out the song, if you've never heard it before), I've devised a recipe that is both sweet and sour - and hopefully will make you come back for more time and time again.

[VOICE-OVER]

These chocolate caramels can also be coated in chocolate for a smoother finish. Dark, milk or white chocolate would all enhance the look. In this case press the balls into a tiny amount of sea salt, just as the chocolate sets.

[MISE-EN-SCENE]

1. Break the chocolate into a heatproof bowl and place over a pan of barely simmering water. Allow to soften, then stir in the coffee.

2. Remove the chocolate from the heat and allow to cool slightly, then stir in the toffee until well combined. Decant into a tub. (If the chocotoffee ribbons happen to meet your fingers on the way feel free to lick them clean but don't forget to wash them before the next step.) Chill until solid.

3. Cover a large plate with a layer of cocoa powder. Crush several pinches of sea salt between your fingers and scatter over the cocoa.

4. Using a melon baller scoop out several chocolate balls. Drop them on to the cocoa and roll them gently around to coat.

5. Place the balls in the fridge until ready. If you really want to suck hard on the chef's salty balls, place in the freezer for 30 minutes before serving.

French Fries

HAPPY DAYS (1974–1984)

'Arnold, go and cook up a couple of burgers for us'
'But I just cleaned the grill'
'Well, good! Then maybe they'll taste better'

[CAST & CREW]

4 to 6 large floury
potatoes
flavourless oil, for
  deep-frying, (you can
  use beef dripping if
  you prefer the flavour)
salt, for sprinkling
tomato ketchup, to serve

Serves 4

Happy Days brought a slice of Americana into our very own living rooms in the 1970s. We were all envious of Richie, Potsie, Ralph Malph, Chachi and the Fonz — teenagers who rode Harleys, played basketball and didn't have to wear school uniform.

Best of all though, this gang of best friends had Al's Diner to hang out, a diner that sold this incredibly good-looking food. A pure slice of the American life — milkshakes, burgers and French fries.

A perfectly cooked chip — crispy on the outside, fluffy on the inside and seasoned with a pinch of salt — is one of the foods handed down by the gods. A simple but truly delectable dish that, in my house, is usually scoffed within seconds.

So cook up a batch, thump the jukebox and indulge.

[VOICE-OVER]

Double-frying chips gives a softer interior and a crispy coating. The blanched chips can also be kept and then fried up as and when needed. Some advocate the thrice-fried chip. If you have the time and the inclination, then please experiment but these chips are just fine only cooked twice.

[MISE-EN-SCENE]

1. Pull your motorbike up to the front of the diner, look at your reflection in the window, run a comb through your hair and swagger through the door.

2. Peel the potatoes carefully, cutting out any eyes and dark marks. Slice into your favourite chip size. (Arnold's Drive-In served thin French fries but if you want fat chips have it your waaayyyyy.) Using kitchen roll pat the excess moisture off the uncooked fries.

3. Pour 10cm (4in) oil into a large pan. Heat to 160°C-170°C, then carefully lower the chips into the oil. Cook until soft but not coloured at all. Drain and cool on kitchen paper.

4. Increase the temperature to 185°C. Return the partly cooked chips to the very hot oil for another minute or so until crispy and golden brown.

5. Drain again on kitchen roll, sprinkle with salt and serve with attitude and a dollop of ketchup on the side.

6. Put your thumbs up and say 'Heyyyyyyy'.

Phoebe's Grandma's Cookies

FRIENDS (1994-2004)

'My grandmother said she got the recipe from her grandmother, Neslay Tolouse'

[CAST & CREW]

225g (7^1/$_2$ oz) plain flour
1 tsp baking soda
1 tsp salt
225g (7^1/$_2$ oz) butter, softened
165g (5^1/$_2$ oz) granulated sugar
150g (5oz) soft brown sugar
1 tsp vanilla extract
2 large eggs
350g (11^1/$_2$ oz) chocolate chips or chopped chocolate
150g (5oz) chopped nuts

Makes 60

This is the one where you get to perfect the recipe that Monica struggled to re-create.

Prized as a family recipe and sworn to secrecy at her grandmother's deathbed, Phoebe cannot share her recipe for the cookies. Monica tries and fails to reproduce the cookies texture and taste for herself.

Phoebe finally explains that the recipe may lie in her French ancestry and her grandmother 'Neslay Tolouse'. The penny drops.

Nestlé Tollhouse (a popular cookie brand) very kindly put the ingredients on the back of every packet!

[VOICE-OVER]

Make this basic recipe unique to your family. Make double chocolate cookies by replacing 50g (2oz) flour with cocoa. White chips, peanut butter chips and even mint choc chips are available. Next time you visit the USA make room in your luggage for a bag or two of these – you might even find a family heirloom written on the packet if you are lucky.

[MISE-EN-SCENE]

1. Preheat the oven to 190°C (170°C) mark 4. Sit your grandmother down for a cup of tea and a chat. Find a suitable notepad and ask her to tell you her cookery secrets. She will be flattered and you will be better fed.

2. Sieve the flour, baking soda and salt into a small bowl.

3. In a larger bowl beat together the butter, sugar and vanilla extract until creamy and paler in colour.

4. Add the eggs, one at a time, beating well after each addition. If the mixture starts to curdle, add 1 tbsp dry mixture. Gradually fold in the remaining mixture. Stir in the chocolate chips or chopped chocolate and the nuts.

5. Place rounded tablespoons of the cookie dough on ungreased baking sheets.

6. Bake for 9-11 minutes until golden brown. Allow to cool for 2 minutes, then place on wire racks to cool completely. If you are not able to wait then wait long enough so that you don't burn your mouth.

Bonus Features

Anyone who has seen the exquisite opening credits to *American Psycho* (2000) will know that food in movies can be suggestive of absolutely anything – from sex to murder. And in the case of *American Psycho*, both.

As you have no doubt gathered by now there are lots of food scenes in movies, many more than we've been able to squeeze into this book. But now you are a committed film-foodie like me, I hope you'll go back and re-watch your favourite movies and spot the scenes where food plays a part. You'll be amazed, as I was, at just how prominent sometimes it can be – from the lunch scene in *The Breakfast Club* (where each detainee's lunch symbolises something about their teenage personality) to a good ol' fashion food fight in *National Lampoon's Animal House*.

Should you wish to delve deeper still into this world then here are just a few more of my favourite movies and their complementary meals...

American Psycho (2000) –
Swordfish meatloaf
with onion marmalade,
rare roasted partridge
breast in raspberry
coulis with a sorrel
timbale

**84 Charing Cross Road
(1987) –**
Yorkshire puddings

In America (2002) –
Colcannon

Layer Cake (2004) –
Sponge cake

**I Love You To Death
(1990) –**
Pizza (watch out for the
poison!)

Hot Fuzz (2007) –
Black Forest Gateau
(Danny's punishment!)

Comfort and Joy (1984) –
A '99' ice cream
(whipped ice cream with
a chocolate flake in a
cone)

The Gold Rush (1925) –
Charlie's boot

**Lady and the Tramp
(1955) –**
Spaghetti (for two)

Fawlty Towers (1975) –
Waldorf salad

**A Christmas Carol (2009)
–** A whole turkey (one
for everyone!)

Ratatouille (2007) –
('It sounds like 'rat'
and 'patootie')
Ratatouille

Taxi Driver (1976) –
Apple pie (with a cheese
crust)

Vera Drake (2004) –
Tea and Biscuits

Calendar Girls (2003) –
Cherry Buns

Scream (1996) –
Popcorn

**Little Miss Sunshine
(2006) –**
Fried chicken and corn

**Mr and Mrs Smith
(2005) –**
Pot roast

Guys and Dolls (1955) –
Cheesecake

Tampopo (1985) –
Ramen noodles

Tortilla Soup (2001) –
Chicken Tortilla Soup

Falling Down (1993) –
Flat hamburgers!

**Once Upon A Time In
Mexico (2003) –**
Cochinita pibil

American Beauty (1999) –
Roasted Asparagus

**There's Something About
Mary (1998) –**
Frank and Beans!

Oscar Acceptance Speech

Thank you! Oh! Thank you! I can hardly believe this! I feel so blessed! And this book — it's so full of pages! Oh, thank you again!

To my family and friends, who have devoured the tastier morsels and scraped the disasters into the bin, I am eternally grateful for their full and frank criticism.

To M, Z and C who have put up with so many bizarre meals for dinner, and not made too much fuss when I needed to use the computer. I return the comfy chair in the study for you to fight over.

To everyone at Portico books, especially Mal, and to Tom Bromley too, I send my astonishment. Not only did they seem to think I might be able to write a book, they were willing to pay me to do it too. In my wildest dreams I have imagined being a food writer and now *Movie Dinners* has helped to make my dreams come true. To all the food writers who have given me inspiration and plenty of bedtime reading, I offer a huge thank you.

To the Studio 123 in Sutton and the ABC Ewell, I'd like to say thanks for providing me with shelter on wet Saturday afternoons as we watched the latest releases. To the Penultimate Picture Palace and the Not the Moulin Rouge in Oxford, I remember the stifled hilarity as we tried to be grown-ups watching art-house movies until we realised the loos were labelled Pearl and Dean.

I'd like to thank every director who included food as a character in their movies. Not only did you give me something to think about when the plot line thinned out but you have inspired me to try some totally new tastes and experiences.

So, thank you, thank you so much, I will treasure this moment forever.

Thank you and good night.

Fin